Anne Woodcock

Joy

Happiness of the Heart

GOOD BOOK GUIDE

7-Session Bible Study

Joy: Happiness of the Heart
A Good Book Guide
© The Good Book Company, 2025.
Published by The Good Book Company

thegoodbook.com | thegoodbook.co.uk
thegoodbook.com.au | thegoodbook.co.nz | thegoodbook.co.in

A CIP catalogue record for this book is available from the British Library.

Design by André Parker and Drew McCall

ISBN: 9781802541007 | JOB-008038 | Printed in India

Contents

# Introduction

One of the Bible writers described God's word as "a lamp for my feet, a light on my path" (Psalm 119:105, NIV). God gave us the Bible to tell us about who he is and what he wants for us. He speaks through it by his Spirit and lights our way through life.

That means that we need to look carefully at the Bible and uncover its meaning—but we also need to apply what we've discovered to our lives.

Good Book Guides are designed to help you do just that. The sessions in this book are interactive and easy to lead. They're perfect for use in groups or for personal study.

Let's take a look at what is included in each session.

Talkabout: Every session starts with an ice-breaker question, designed to get people talking around a subject that links to the Bible study.

Investigate: These questions help you explore what the passage is about.

Apply: These questions are designed to get you thinking practically: what does this Bible teaching mean for you and your church?

Explore More: These optional sections help you to go deeper or to explore another part of the Bible which connects with the main passage.

Getting Personal: These sections are a chance for personal reflection. Some groups may feel comfortable discussing these, but you may prefer to look at them quietly as individuals instead—or leave them out.

Pray: Here, you're invited to pray in the light of the truths and challenges you've seen in the study.

Each session is also designed to be easily split into two! Watch out for the **Apply** section that comes halfway through, and stop there if you haven't got time to do the whole thing in one go.

In the back of the book, you'll find a **Leader's Guide**, which provides helpful notes on every question, along with everything else that group leaders need in order to facilitate a great session and help the group uncover the riches of God's light-giving word.

Why Study Joy?

A guide to *joy*? Can there be such a thing? Isn't the experience of joy in fact rather like hiccupping—there's no sure-fire way to make or help ourselves do it or feel it? It just happens. So, if joy is only a spontaneous reaction to a delightful situation, and our circumstances are not delightful, how are we meant to rejoice?

But God's word takes a different view. Many times the Old Testament exhorts God's people to shout, sing and celebrate God, his deeds and his words with joy. And joy is constantly called for and expected in the lives of Jesus' followers, and on display even as they endure tough situations.

These seven studies take readers on a Bible journey through the Christian life—from first understanding God's revelation to us in his word, through the repentance and faith that bring us into the kingdom of God, and then looking at our redeemed relationships with the Lord and with his people, as well as our redeemed experience of trials and suffering in this world, to the hope promised to all who persevere faithfully to the end—all the while showing us the whys and hows of cultivating deep and resilient joy in all circumstances.

Beginning with Paul's counterintuitive instruction to the Christians at Philippi to rejoice in the Lord always, these studies have been written in the prayerful hope that each reader will be strengthened to gladly obey this "impossible" command as they faithfully follow the only one who can give us everlasting joy.

The Command to Rejoice

Philippians 3:17 - 4:9

Talkabout

1. Think of a time when you rejoiced about something. Briefly describe it. How did you feel? How did you express those feelings? What was the reason? Do you feel that joy now? How long did it last?

Investigate

Philippians 4:4 is one of the best-known Bible verses about being joyful. It's found towards the end of Paul's letter to the church in Philippi, which had been established as a result of his visit there with Silas (see Acts 16).

📖 **Read Philippians 3:17 – 4:9**

DICTIONARY

Brothers and sisters (3:17): fellow Christians.
Their glory (v 19): what they prize most.
Crown (4:1): a garland, often of laurel leaves, awarded in ancient Greece to a winning athlete.

Whose names are in the book of life (v 3): those who through faith belong to Christ (Revelation 13:8) and will be saved from God's wrath on the day of judgment (20:11-15).
Transcends (Philippians 4:7): goes beyond; trumps.

---

2. Reread Philippians 4:4. This is not a request, a suggestion or even strong advice. It's a command! Given the subject, why might some people find this surprising or difficult?

- What does this tell us about how Paul views rejoicing?

3. What are believers to rejoice in here? And how much?

- How are the reason for our joy and the frequency of our joy connected?

4. What does Paul instruct his readers to do both at the beginning and the end of this passage (3:17; 4:9)?

- Paul's command to rejoice comes between these two instructions to follow his example, and the rest of the letter mentions his joy in a variety of difficult circumstances (see Explore More). How could this change our view of rejoicing?

5. What situation in Philippi does Paul highlight immediately before he commands the Philippians to rejoice in the Lord (4:2-3)? And what problem does he mention following that command (v 6)?

- Clearly the situation in Philippi wasn't perfect or easy. So what do these verses tell us about how Paul views joy?

- If we are anxious about our lack of joy, what should we do?

Explore More | OPTIONAL

Paul's letter tells us a lot about both the causes of his joy and the obstacles to rejoicing that he faced.

- What specific things is Paul rejoicing in as he writes to the Philippians?
  - 1:4-6
  - 1:18
  - 2:16-17
  - 4:10, 15-18

- What obstacles to rejoicing is Paul facing (or has he faced) as he writes? And what emotions could these situations generate that could threaten to undermine Paul's joy?
  - 1:12-14, 20
  - 1:15, 17
  - 3:2, 18
  - 4:12-15

Apply

6. What is it that most gives you joy? And how permanent is that joy? Could it be described as rejoicing in the Lord?

* What have you learned so far in Philippians that would help you to grow in rejoicing in the Lord always?

Getting Personal | OPTIONAL

Reflect on who Jesus is and what he does for his people.

"The Lord Jesus Christ … by the power that enables him to bring everything under his control, will transform our lowly bodies so that they will be like his glorious body." (Philippians 3:20-21)

"The Lord is near." (4:5)

"My God will meet all your needs according to the riches of his glory in Christ Jesus." (4:19)

Which of those truths gives you most joy?

Investigate

We've seen that Paul commands believers to rejoice. That may feel like a tall order! Let's look at some verses that show us how it's possible.

7. Read Galatians 5:22-23. What are the implications of Galatians 5:22 for how we think about joy as Christian believers?

- How does this make it possible to "rejoice … always", even in hard circumstances (Philippians 4:4)?

8. Read Romans 8:5-6. Look at what Paul says about a believer's mind. What similar things does he say about our minds in the Philippians passage?
   - Philippians 3:18-21

   - 4:8

9. How does all this (from questions 7 and 8) help us in following Paul's command to "rejoice in the Lord always"? What should we seek to do if we want to rejoice more?

10. In the Bible, commands are given in the context of truth about God and promises from God. What truth (Philippians 4:5) and what promise (v 7) accompany this command?

   - How are the two connected?

- What do we need to do that will enable us to rejoice in the Lord always?

Apply

11. How have you seen the work of the Holy Spirit in your life, especially in growing the fruit of joy in you?

Pray

"Rejoice always, pray continually, give thanks in all circumstances; for this is God's will for you in Christ Jesus. Do not quench the Spirit."
(1 Thessalonians 5:16-19)

Spend time rejoicing in the Lord together, thanking and praising him for who he is and what he has done.

Pray for the help of the Holy Spirit to grow joy and gratitude in you so that you will rejoice in the Lord always.

2

Joy in Understanding God's Revelation

Nehemiah 7:73 – 8:12; Luke 10:17-24

Talkabout

1. Share about a time when "the light dawned" and you understood something clearly for the first time (a subject at school, how to fix something, a sport or creative skill, realising how your significant other felt about you, etc.).

   - Share about a time when "the light dawned" in your life as a follower of Jesus, and you understood something clearly about him in a new and powerful way.

The Christian life has many of these "light dawning" moments. Wonderfully, God reveals his truth to us not merely for our information but for our joy. In this study we'll look at an example of this from both the Old and New Testaments.

Investigate

Nehemiah tells us about events in Israel (aka Judah) towards the end of the Old Testament history of God's people. Because of their rebellion against God, they had spent 70 years in exile after defeat by the Babylonians, who were later themselves defeated by the Persians—just as God promised. The Persian emperor Cyrus then permitted God's people to return to their land—again, just as God promised—leading to the following event in Nehemiah.

📖 **Read Nehemiah 7:73 – 8:12**

DICTIONARY

Levites (8:7): descendants of Levi who were given the responsibility of looking after the tabernacle/temple and helping the priests, including assisting with teaching the law.

---

2. What was the purpose of this gathering (v 1)?

- Read Isaiah 49:6. How is this event in Nehemiah part of the fulfilment of God's promise to make his restored people "a light for the Gentiles"?

3. What point is made repeatedly throughout this passage (Nehemiah 8:2, 3, 8, 12)?

- How was the law of God taught (v 2-4, 5-6, 7-8)?

- How did the people respond to this opportunity (v 3)?

4. What effect did hearing the law of God have on the listeners initially (v 9)?

- Why, do you think? (Skim-read the Israelites' prayer in 9:5-35.)

5. How did the leaders intervene (8:9-11)? Why?

6. Look again at verse 12. Why did the people's response change?

- How did they express joy?

Grief over our sin is an appropriate response to God's word—but it should always lead us to joy at God's kindness and character.

Apply

7. What emotional response do you typically associate with hearing God's word taught, and why?

- What practical lessons can we learn from this true story about how to find joy in God's truth?

Getting Personal | OPTIONAL

"Do not grieve, for the joy of the LORD is your strength." (v 10)

When we move beyond rightful fear of God's holiness to a personal appreciation of his love, grace, and forgiveness for sinners like us, we are strengthened to be patient in hope, endure suffering, resist temptation, stay faithful in persecution and find energy to serve him.

Is there something in your walk with God that you are grieving over right now? If so, ask the Lord to help you also feel joy in who he is and what he has done for sinners, as revealed in Scripture, so that you are strengthened to live for him.

Investigate

We now turn to Luke 10, where Jesus has recently sent out 72 disciples in pairs ahead of him to proclaim the kingdom of God and do miracles in his name (v 1-16).

📖 Read Luke 10:17-24

DICTIONARY

Little children (v 21): disciples of Jesus (see 18:16).

This passage is one of only two in the New Testament that mention the joy of Jesus.

8. What was it, specifically, that gave Jesus joy (v 21-24)?

9. What humbling truth is revealed here about our understanding of God? How should we view ourselves?

10. What exciting truth is revealed here about God's attitude to us in our ignorance? How should we respond?

If you are a Christian, you are a little one to whom God has revealed himself—and he continues to reveal himself to you as you read his word. That is surely a cause for joy!

Apply

11. The fact that God reveals his truth to Jesus' disciples causes Jesus to "jump for joy"! This revelation is also available to us in Scripture (Ephesians 3:2-6). In fact, it is the foundation of the whole church (2:19-20). How will this affect the way you approach God's word and respond to it?

Explore More | OPTIONAL

📖 Reread Luke 10:17-20

- How does the disciples' reason for joy (v 17) differ from what Jesus wants them to rejoice in (v 20)?

The image of a heavenly book or scroll with names "written" in it occurs throughout the Old Testament.

- What do the following verses reveal about it?
  - Exodus 32:31-33
  - Psalm 69:28
  - Daniel 12:1
  - Malachi 3:16-18

- What are the implications of our names being written in heaven?
- How is Jesus' reason for joy a better one than the disciples', do you think?
- The disciples overlook that reason for joy, and so might we. Why, do you think?

Pray

"We declare God's wisdom, a mystery that has been hidden and that God destined for our glory before time began. None of the rulers of this age understood it, for if they had, they would not have crucified the Lord of glory. However, as it is written: 'What no eye has seen, what no ear has heard, and what no human mind has conceived'—the things God has prepared for those who love him—these are the things God has revealed to us by his Spirit." (1 Corinthians 2:7-10, quoting Isaiah 64:4)

Think of as many things as you can that "God has prepared for those who love him"—truths and promises that you have discovered in his word, revealed to you by his Spirit. Spend time giving thanks to him—with joy!

3

Joy in Repentance and Faith

Acts 16:16-34; Psalm 51

Talkabout

1. What was it that gave you joy when you first turned to the Lord Jesus Christ in repentance and faith? (Or, if you grew up in a Christian family, when did your repentance and faith first lead to joy and why?)

Investigate

In Acts 16 we read Luke's account of what happened when Paul and Silas first visited the city of Philippi. These events led to the establishment of the Philippian church, to whom Paul later wrote his letter.

📖 Read Acts 16:16-34

DICTIONARY

Baptised (v 33): being symbolically washed in water as a public sign of repentance and faith in Jesus Christ and joining his church.

---

2. Why were Paul and Silas thrown into prison?

- What obstacles had they encountered that might have dampened their joy?

3. What reasons can you think of to explain why—despite all that had happened—Paul and Silas could pray and sing hymns to God in prison? (See also Acts 5:41-42; 7:59-60; 13:49-52.)

4. What was the effect of Paul and Silas's actions on the other prisoners (16:25, 28)?

5. What immediate danger was the jailer facing, which might have provoked his question to Paul and Silas (v 30)?

- What evidence is there to suggest that his question was in fact a spiritual one?

6. What's the evidence that the jailer responded to Paul's teaching both in repentance and faith?

- What effect did this have on the jailer himself, and how did that contrast with the way he had felt previously?

7. What hints does the story give about how the jailer's life would change from now on (v 32-34)?

Apply

8. The jailer was "filled with joy because he had come to believe in God" (v 34). Why might this be a surprising statement to some who don't follow the Lord Jesus Christ?

- Why don't unbelievers equate repenting and trusting in Jesus with joy? Is there anything believers could do to remedy this? What could you do?

Getting Personal | OPTIONAL

"I tell you, there is rejoicing in the presence of the angels of God over one sinner who repents." (Luke 15:10)

Who is rejoicing here? Someone in the presence of the angels of God—surely the Lord himself. That's what we see in the story that follows: the father celebrating the return of his long-lost son.

How do you feel when you realise that your repentance and faith caused a celebration in heaven itself?

Investigate

Repentance and faith isn't just something that gives us joy when we begin the Christian life; it's a repeated pattern that continues to bring us joy as we go on in the Christian life.

Israel's King David, though commended as "a man after [God's] own heart" (Acts 13:22), certainly didn't live a perfect life. At one point he sinned grievously by committing adultery and murdering the unsuspecting husband to cover up his sin (2 Samuel 11 – 12). After God had used the prophet Nathan to open David's eyes to his own wrongdoing, David wrote Psalm 51 to express his repentance and renewed faith in the Lord.

📖 **Read Psalm 51**

DICTIONARY

Transgressions (v 1, 3) and **iniquity** (v 2, 9): sin.
Hyssop (v 7): a herb connected with blood and cleansing in Old Testament animal sacrifices.

Burnt offerings (v 16, 19): an animal sacrifice in which the whole animal was burned up; alongside the sin offering it atoned for sin (Leviticus 1; 9:7; Numbers 28:3-4).
Zion (v 18): Jerusalem.

9. What has David discovered about himself (v 1-6)? Try to find at least five things.

10. What will bring David joy again (v 7-12)? Try to find at least five things.

- What part does David play in any of this?

11. According to David, what does God delight in (v 13-19)?

Explore More | OPTIONAL

Once David had repented of his sin and trusted in God to restore him, he could again worship God in the way God had prescribed—through animal sacrifices such as burnt offerings—and be confident of God's delight in those sacrifices (v 16-19). That was part of David's restored joy (v 12).

📖 **Read 1 John 1:5 – 2:2**

- What is different for God's people today?
- What remains the same for God's people today?
- What reasons for even greater joy than David's does this passage give us?

Apply

12. As believers in Jesus, what have we learned from Psalm 51 about how our joy can be lost but also restored?

- Consider the three "movements" we've observed in Psalm 51:
  1) owning our sin without excuses
  2) seeking forgiveness from the Lord
  3) trusting him to accept our repentance and delight in us

  Which of those do you tend to struggle with most? Which verse from Psalm 51 would it be most helpful to hold on to in those moments?

Pray

"Restore to me the joy of your salvation." (v 11-12)

Where are you in this psalm right now?

- *Are you feeling crushed and unclean over your sin (v 7-8)? Pray David's prayer for yourself.*

- *Have you brought the sacrifice of a broken and contrite heart to the Lord (v 17)? Know that God will not despise it.*

- *Are you filled with the joy of your salvation (v 12)? Declare God's praises.*

Are none of these true of you? Ask God to speak to you through this psalm and the testimonies of others (v 13) so that you too can discover joy in repentance and faith.

4

Joy in the Lord

John 15:26 - 16:24

Talkabout

1. Share about a reunion with a loved one. What happened when you first met up? What had you most missed about them? What was different between video calls and seeing them face to face?

Investigate

In session 1 Paul commanded us to "rejoice in the Lord" (Philippians 4:4). In this session we'll consider more about what it means to rejoice in Jesus.

We pick up John's Gospel on the night before Jesus dies. He has told the disciples (minus Judas) that he will not be with them for much longer; he will soon leave them (e.g. 13:33; 14:2-4, 28-29). Although the disciples are unaware of it, Jesus actually has two "departures" in view: his death, and his ascension to his Father in heaven. Yet while the disciples' understanding is incomplete, their grief is real; so in this passage, Jesus starts to address the sadness that the disciples are already feeling.

📖 Read John 15:26 – 16:15

DICTIONARY

Advocate (15:26): helper, comforter.
Testify (v 26): tell the truth.

Synagogue (16:2): local Jewish religious assembly.

2. What is Jesus' purpose in speaking to his disciples at this time (16:1)?

- What purpose has he previously mentioned in 15:11? How are the two purposes related?

- To this end, what mission (15:27), promise (v 26) and warning (16:2) does Jesus give the disciples?

3. At this point, what do the disciples understand (16:5) and not understand (v 6-7)?

- Why are they filled with grief?

4. In what counterintuitive way does Jesus address their grief (v 7)?

5. What will the Spirit do when he comes (v 8-11)?

The Spirit's proof to the world (v 8-11) is connected to Jesus "going away" (v 7)—here, that means his death, resurrection and ascension.

6. Why, then, must Jesus "leave" before the Spirit can come?

7. How does Jesus say the Spirit will help these specific disciples, and how will that help them in their grief (v 12-15)?

Apply

8. When might you be tempted to regret Jesus' physical absence from this world?

- But what would be missing today if Jesus had not physically left us?

- Can you think of a time when, through the Spirit, you've particularly felt Jesus near? How did that bring you joy?

Explore More | OPTIONAL

Deep intimate joy is at the heart of the relationship that God seeks to have with his people. This is why, throughout the Bible, his gift of marriage illustrates first the relationship between himself and his people (Israel) and then Jesus and his people (the church). Let's look at one example.

📖 Read Song of Songs 1:1-4

The song celebrates the love story of a great king and a woman who is something of a Cinderella. She begins the song and is then accompanied by friends in verse 4.

- How is the woman's joy expressed here? Where does it rank between feeling okay and ecstatic?
- What is the source of joy in these verses—both of the woman and the chorus of friends?
- How does this speak to the relationship between Jesus and his people? (See Luke 24:27.)
- Do we have as much joy in Jesus as this woman has in her lover? If not, what might be the problem?
- How can we rekindle love for the Lord?

Investigate

Jesus has been talking about his "going away". In 15:26 – 16:15, it was ultimately his ascension that was mainly in view. In 16:16, he switches to speaking about his death. Unsurprisingly, the disciples are confused…

📖 Read John 16:16-24

9. Reread Jesus' statement in verse 16. Which of his words particularly perplex the disciples and why, do you think?

10. Jesus is preparing the disciples for his crucifixion by promising them joy (see column 1 in the table below). What four things do we learn about the joy that Jesus promises? (Complete column 2.)

John 16	Promise	NT Reference	Fulfilment
v 20		John 20:19-20	
v 21		1 Peter 2:24	
v 22		Romans 6:5-10	
v 24		Philippians 4:4-7	

- Later in the New Testament, how do we see Jesus' promises to his disciples regarding joy come true? (From the verses in column 3, complete column 4.)

11. Read Luke 24:50-52. How does Jesus' promise of joy come true just 40 days after his resurrection?

• Why is the disciples' joy here surprising, and why not?

Apply

12. What have you learned from this passage that fuels your joy?

• Where else, other than in the Lord, are you likely to look for joy? How does that compare with joy in Jesus?

• How could the truths from this study help you the next time you feel that you have lost your joy?

Getting Personal | OPTIONAL

"Though you have not seen him, you love him; and even though you do not see him now, you believe in him and are filled with an inexpressible and glorious joy." (1 Peter 1:8)

Is this true of you? Is your greatest joy in knowing and loving him and knowing that he knows and loves you? Of course, many wonderful things in this life rightly give us joy: family, friends, work, hobbies, church, travel, nature, books, art, music, ideas... But do you have joy that nothing and no one can remove—joy in Jesus himself?

Pray

"My Father will give you whatever you ask in my name ... Ask and you will receive, and your joy will be complete." (John 16:23-24)

What can you ask for in Jesus' name from your heavenly Father?

5

Joy in Christ's Body

Acts 2:36-47; 1 Thessalonians 2:17 - 3:13

Talkabout

1. Why do you think people get so excited about the atmosphere at events where there's a large crowd? What makes experiences more enjoyable when we share them with others?

The New Testament is clear that our gatherings as a church are meant to have a distinct atmosphere too—a joyful one!

Investigate

At Pentecost, when Peter preached in Jerusalem in the power of the Holy Spirit, the church immediately grew from about 120 believers (Acts 1:15) to more than 3,000 (2:41). In Acts 2, Luke describes the life of these believers together as they formed the first church.

📖 **Read Acts 2:36-47**

Messiah (v 36): the rescuer God promised throughout the Old Testament to send to his people.
Apostles (v 37): men appointed by Jesus to testify about him.

Fellowship (v 42): sharing together as those who have much in common.
The breaking of bread (v 42, 46): the Lord's Supper (1 Corinthians 11:23-26) and eating together.

2. What had the people who formed the first church experienced in common with each other (v 36-41)?

- What does this role-model church teach us about what should happen next when an individual accepts the gospel?

- What does it teach us about what a church is—and who belongs to it?

3. What four characteristics of a church are listed here (v 42)?

- What was the attitude of the believers to these things (beginning of verse 42)?

4. How did the believers express their fellowship (v 44-46)?

- How did they feel about their fellowship?

Explore More | OPTIONAL

📖 Read 1 John 1:1-4

In this letter the apostle John begins by proclaiming that Jesus—whom John has seen and heard and touched "in the flesh"—is the Word of life and eternal life, who was with God the Father and has appeared to the apostles.

- What is John's goal for his readers in proclaiming this (beginning of verse 3)?

But he doesn't stop there!

- What other fellowship is produced by this message (end of verse 3)?
- What is going to make John joyful?

Apply

5. How much would your fellowship with other believers in your church be recognisable to these New Testament believers, do you think? What are the differences?

- Is there anything you can do to help people in your church grow closer to resembling this first church?

6. In what ways does your fellowship with other believers in your church make you sincerely glad?

- If this is lacking, might that be because you need to invest more in your fellowship? If so, how could you do that?

Getting Personal | OPTIONAL

"Do not be yoked together with unbelievers. For what do righteousness and wickedness have in common? Or what fellowship can light have with darkness? … Or what does a believer have in common with an unbeliever?" (2 Corinthians 6:14-15)

Paul is very clear: if, after they've become a Christian, a believer then chooses to form close connections with unbelievers instead of with fellow believers, that signals that something is wrong.

Is this you in any way? If yes, seek help—from the Lord and from his people. If it sounds like someone you know, pray for them and think about how to help them. (See 1 Corinthians 7:12-13, 15-16; 1 Peter 3:1-4 for Bible wisdom to help those already in mixed marriages.)

Investigate

We get another glimpse of the joy that comes from fellowship with God's people in the apostle Paul's first letter to the Thessalonians. Paul was probably in Thessalonica for only about three weeks (see Acts 17), but as a result of his visit, a church was formed—one which had a special place in his heart, as we shall see.

📖 **Read 1 Thessalonians 2:17 – 3:13**

Crown (2:19): laurel wreath placed on the head of a champion athlete.
Trials (3:3): tough times.

The tempter (v 5): the devil.
Holy ones (v 13): followers of Jesus who have already died (see 4:14-16).

7. How many times does Paul mention "joy" in this passage?

- What exactly gives him joy?

8. Paul's joy results from his hope. What hope is he looking forward to, and where do the Thessalonian believers fit in (2:19-20; 3:13)?

9. Paul's joy results from his faith—in "our God and Father … and our Lord Jesus" (v 11). What does he trust the Lord to do (v 8-13)?

- What thieves of joy does his faith overcome (v 2-5)?

10. Paul's joy is linked with his love for the Thessalonian believers. How does he express that here (2:17, 19-20; 3:5, 8, 9, 12)?

11. How has Paul invested in his fellowship with the Thessalonian believers (2:17; 3:1-2 and 5-6, 10-13)?

Apply

12. How do you think your fellowship with other believers compares with that of Paul and the Thessalonians? How much is it based on the faith, hope and love that are ours in Christ? (Or does it centre around something else?)

• Paul seems to have written his letter from Athens (3:1); the fellowship of believers from whom he was separated was very important to him. How could you grow in fellowship with believers who live elsewhere?

Pray

"How can we thank God enough for you in return for all the joy we have in the presence of our God because of you?" (v 9)

Is there anyone about whom you can say what Paul says here about the Thessalonian believers?

• *If yes, spend time thanking God for his gift of fellowship to you.*

• *If no, ask God to help you find joy in fellowship with Christian brothers and sisters.*

6

Joy in Suffering

Luke 6:17-36

Talkabout

1. Think of a time when you persisted with something that was painful or stressful because you knew that the outcome would make it all worthwhile. How did you feel along the way and in the end?

Investigate

Luke's account of Jesus' teaching in Luke 6 is known as the Sermon on the Plain (see v 17). There are similarities with the Sermon on the Mount recorded in Matthew's Gospel (e.g. v 20-23; compare Matthew 5:3-12) but also some differences (see Luke 6:24-26, not mentioned in Matthew).

📖 Read Luke 6:17-26

DICTIONARY

Blessed (v 20-22): happy—even enviable.
Kingdom of God (v 20): here, salvation and eternal life in God's paradise.
Son of Man (v 22): a title Jesus used to refer to himself (see Daniel 7:13-14).

Prophets (v 23): men from Israel's history who proclaimed God's word, especially promises of the coming Messiah.
Woe (v 24-26): a warning of future trouble and distress.

2. Look at the description of Jesus' ministry in verses 17-19. What might people expect life to be like for Jesus' disciples?

3. What does *Jesus* expect life to be like for his disciples (v 20-23)?

- List all the kinds of suffering that he mentions.

4. According to Jesus, in what ways are his disciples blessed amid all this suffering?

- How does Jesus describe their joy in looking forward to their reward in heaven (v 26)?

5. Jesus' followers will be helped to persevere through suffering by keeping their future in view. What view of the past will help them too (v 26)?

6. Jesus' disciples have a focus on the future. What is the focus for those in verses 24-26? And so, what is the chief characteristic that Jesus is looking for here?

- Why should we not envy the people described in verses 24-26?

Explore More | OPTIONAL

- How does the writer of the book of Hebrews make the same point as Jesus in Luke 6?
  - Hebrews 10:32-39
  - Hebrews 12:2-3
  - Hebrews 12:16-17
  - Hebrews 13:11-14

Apply

7. How are you encouraged to persevere in faithfulness to the Lord through tough times by looking back to history (including Bible history) or looking forward to eternity? Talk about any people and events (from the past) or promises (for the future) that have particularly helped you.

Investigate

📖 **Read Luke 6:27-36**

DICTIONARY

Sinners (v 32): here, those who are judged as bad people in society.

---

8. Jesus is speaking these words to "you who are listening" (v 27). Who are these people (v 20) and can you summarise Jesus' message to them in one sentence?

9. What practical differences can be seen in someone's life when they trust Jesus' assurance that his followers are blessed in suffering?

10. What is the ultimate reward that they will receive (v 35-36)?

Apply

11. "To you who are listening I say…" (v 27). What is it that stops us from truly listening to Jesus in this area?

- Why might we struggle to trust that we are blessed when we are suffering for him?

- Why might we feel unable to be kind to the ungrateful and wicked, as our heavenly Father is?

- How are we helped by doing these things alongside one another?

Getting Personal | OPTIONAL

"Consider it pure joy, my brothers and sisters, whenever you face trials of many kinds, because you know that the testing of your faith produces perseverance … Blessed is the one who perseveres under trial because, having stood the test, that person will receive the crown of life that the Lord has promised to those who love him." (James 1:2-4, 12)

Think about the trials you are facing right now. If "pure joy" were the North Pole, whereabouts on Planet Earth would you be?

Then think about the crown of life and the Lord who has promised it to his faithful followers. Plan how to set your mind on these things when trials are eroding your perseverance.

Pray

"Weeping may stay for the night, but rejoicing comes in the morning."
(Psalm 30:5)

Spend some time praying for situations, near or far, in which Christians are suffering a night of weeping because of persecution for their faith. Pray that these brothers and sisters would know the truths highlighted in this study and, as Jesus promises, "leap for joy".

7

Joy in Hope

1 Thessalonians 4:13-18; Revelation 7:9-17

Talkabout

1. In what different ways do people in your culture hope they will "live on" after their death? How well or badly are these hopes likely to fare?

The New Testament holds out a greater hope to believers: life with God for ever. To treasure this hope for the future is the sure recipe for indestructible joy in the present.

Investigate

📖 **Read 1 Thessalonians 4:13-18**

DICTIONARY

Asleep (v 13, 14, 15): here, Paul means believers who have died. This is not true death but only a temporary state in which our bodies await resurrection (John 11:25-26).

Archangel (v 16): a superior rank of angel.

---

2. What concern among the Thessalonian believers is Paul addressing here?

3. List all the things that Paul mentions will take place when the Lord Jesus returns.

4. Therefore, what should differentiate believers in Christ from unbelievers?

- How is the joy experienced by unbelievers undermined by their lack of hope?

Apply

5. When and where have you witnessed hope-filled joy among Christians in the face of death? What effect did it have on others?

Investigate

📖 **Read Revelation 7:9-17**

DICTIONARY

The Lamb (v 9, 10, 14, 17): Jesus (see 5:1-10).
Palm branches (v 9): tokens of joy and triumph for Jewish people, to be waved and strewn on the ground at festivities.

Elders (v 11, 13): 24 of them, representing all the people of God throughout history (see 4:4, 9-11).
Four living creatures (v 11): they represent all of creation (see 4:6-8).
Tribulation (v 14): great trouble and suffering.

---

6. What key things does John tell us about the people of God in eternity (v 9)?

- How can these things cause us joy now, as we wait for this reality to arrive?

7. What do the two songs or declarations (v 10 and 12) reveal about the reasons for joy in eternity?

8. Compare what we are told about life for God's people in this world (7:14) with how their life in eternity is pictured (v 15-17).
   - What is different?

- What is the same?

Explore More | OPTIONAL

The final sentence of verse 17—"God will wipe away every tear from their eyes"—is a quotation from Isaiah 25:8.

📖 **Read Isaiah 25:7-9**

- Look at what God will do, and where (v 7-8a; 24:23). What does this add to our understanding of God wiping away our tears?

---

9. What two relationships are central to John's vision of God's people in eternity (v 17)? What do you find particularly striking about them?

Apply

10. Read 2 Corinthians 4:16-18. Our hope of eternal glory far outweighs our troubles and makes them seem light and momentary. How can we help each other to remember our hope so that we persevere in the faith with joy, even in troubles?

Getting Personal | OPTIONAL

"'Look, I am coming soon! My reward is with me, and I will give to each person according to what they have done' ... The Spirit and the bride [the church] say, 'Come!' And let the one who hears say, 'Come!' Let the one who is thirsty come; and let the one who wishes take the free gift of the water of life." (Revelation 22:12, 17)

Think about the return of the Lord Jesus. Is "Come, Lord Jesus" a prayer you pray regularly? Occasionally? Never? What could your answer tell you about where you find your joy? Is there any change you need to make, starting now?

---

11. As this is the final session, spend a few moments writing down and then sharing what has given you most joy in learning about joy over these studies.

Pray

"To him who is able to keep you from stumbling and to present you before his glorious presence without fault and with great joy—to the only God our Saviour be glory, majesty, power and authority, through Jesus Christ our Lord, before all ages, now and for evermore! Amen." (Jude 1:24-25)

Give thanks to God for the great hope set before us and the joy it gives us. And pray for each other—that all of you will remain, with joy, in the eternal safekeeping of God our Saviour and Jesus Christ our Lord.

Joy

Happiness of the Heart

LEADER'S GUIDE

Leader's Guide: Introduction

This Leader's Guide includes guidance for every question. It will provide background information and help you if you get stuck. For each session, you'll also find the following:

The Big Idea: The main point of the session, in brief. This is what you should be aiming to have fixed in people's minds by the end of the session!

Summary: An overview of the passage you're reading together.

Optional Extra: Usually this is an introductory activity that ties in with the main theme of the Bible study and is designed to break the ice at the beginning of a session. Or it may be a "homework project" that people can tackle during the week.

Occasionally the Leader's Guide includes an extra follow-up question, printed in *italics*. This doesn't appear in the main study guide but could be a useful add-on to help your group get to the answer or go deeper.

Here are a few key principles to bear in mind as you prepare to lead:

- Don't just read out the answers from the Leader's Guide. Ideally, you want the group to discover these answers from the Bible for themselves.

- Keep drawing people back to the passage you're studying. People may come up with answers based on their experiences or on teaching they've heard in the past, but the point of this study is to listen to God's word itself—so keep directing your group to look at the text.

- Make sure everyone finishes the session knowing how the passage is relevant for them. We do Bible study so that our lives can be changed by what we hear from God's word. So, **Apply** questions aren't just an add-on—they're a vital part of the session.

Finally, remember that your group is unique! You should feel free to use this Good Book Guide in a way that works for them. If they're a quiet bunch, you might want to spend longer on the **Talkabout** question. If they love to get creative, try using mind-mapping or doodling to kick-start some of your discussions. If your time is limited, you can choose to skip **Explore More** or split the whole session into two. Adapt the material in whatever way you think will help your group get the most out of God's word.

1

The Command to Rejoice
Philippians 3:17 - 4:9

The Big Idea

Joy is both commanded of us as believers and grown in us as part of the fruit of the Spirit, as we set our minds on the Lord, in prayerful dependence on God.

Summary

The big surprise at the beginning of these Bible studies on joy is the apostle Paul's command to rejoice in Philippians 4:4. The verb "rejoice" is not a request, a suggestion or even strong advice but an order (do this!), given twice. This completely contradicts how most people view joy: as a powerful emotion that comes to you unsolicited—a spontaneous reaction to a pleasing situation. If your circumstances are not pleasing, how can you rejoice? And so how can anyone command you to?

But Paul isn't talking about any old joy. Our joy is to be "in the Lord", and it's that reason for our joy that enables us to rejoice with the frequency that Paul commands: "always". Paul makes clear in this letter that the Colossian believers should follow the example of himself and the other apostles (e.g. 3:17; 4:9). Joy is infectious and can be learned from others.

The verses surrounding Paul's command to rejoice mention conflict in the church and also anxiety, underlining how joy is found *in* but not *because of* our circumstances. The Explore More section surveys the various difficult circumstances that Paul mentions in Philippians alongside telling us why he can rejoice in them.

The second part of the study looks at the roles of the Spirit and of our mind (the two are connected) in producing joy in us, along with promises that accompany Paul's command. This first session challenges people to rejoice "in the Lord", to see that this kind of joy can be found in all circumstances, and to learn biblical ways of growing the fruit of joy: by depending on the Spirit, setting our minds on what the Spirit desires, seeking to imitate those around us who display the fruit of joy, remembering all that the Lord is and has done for us, and trusting his promises of continual nearness and the peace that transcends all understanding.

Optional Extra

Turn your first get-together into a joyful celebration of your group. Provide celebratory food and drinks, decorate with balloons or flowers, and have some joyous-sounding music playing as people arrive. Before you start the Bible study, explain why you rejoice in this group and meeting. This will be easier if you already know group members. However, if the group is new to you and each other, be more aspirational instead: tell them what you are looking forward to and hope to celebrate with them by the end of the studies.

Guidance for Questions

1. **Think of a time when you rejoiced about something. Briefly describe it. How did you feel? How did you express those feelings? What was the reason? Do you feel that joy now? How long did it last?**

   Encourage people to share happy memories and to enjoy talking about joy.

2. **Reread Philippians 4:4. This is not a request, a suggestion or even strong advice. It's a command! Given the subject, why might some people find this surprising or difficult?**

   People tend to think of joy as a powerful emotion that comes to you unsolicited—as a spontaneous reaction to a pleasing situation. Paul's command to rejoice requires us to feel joyful, but how can we set out to feel that way?

- **What does this tell us about how Paul views rejoicing?**

   If Paul is commanding believers to rejoice, he can't view joy purely as a spontaneous emotional response. There must be some other characteristic of joy—one which our culture doesn't recognise perhaps—which means we can do something that will result in it. It must be possible to set out to obey the command.

3. **What are believers to rejoice in here? And how much?**

   Paul commands us to rejoice "in the Lord" and to do that "always".

- **How are the reason for our joy and the frequency of our joy connected?**

   We are called to rejoice always because we rejoice in the Lord, who is supremely delightful for his people and the one who never changes (Hebrews 13:8). Perhaps get your group to think of things that are always true of the Lord, meaning that there is never a moment when we can't rejoice in him. For example: the Lord is near (Philippians 4:5); he will never leave us or forsake us; if the Lord is our helper, no one else can do us any harm; he is the same yesterday, today and for ever (Hebrews 13:5, 6, 8).

   And since he is completely faithful, that means that our righteousness, protection from the evil one, hope, forgiveness and purification are all certain (1 Thessalonians 5:23-24; 2 Thessalonians 3:3; Hebrews 10:23; 1 John 1:9). He is never tired or forgetful, and nor will he be overpowered, manipulated or deceived into abandoning or rejecting us. And so on.

4. **What does Paul instruct his readers to do both at the beginning and the end of this passage (3:17; 4:9)?**

   To follow his example. In 3:17 Paul's use of "us" and "we" suggests that he has all the apostles in mind as models for the believers to follow. (See also 1 Corinthians 11:1 and 2 Thessalonians 3:7.)

- **Paul's command to rejoice comes between these two instructions to** follow his example, and the rest of the letter mentions his joy in a variety of difficult circumstances (see Explore More). How could this change our view of rejoicing?

Paul expects the Philippian believers to follow his example. One way they can do that is by rejoicing even in tough situations, as Paul demonstrates throughout the letter. So joy is something that can be learned from others. We could say that it's infectious.

5. **What situation in Philippi does Paul highlight immediately before he commands the Philippians to rejoice in the Lord (4:2-3)? And what problem does he mention following that command (v 6)?**
   - 4:2-3—A conflict has arisen between two of Paul's co-workers, Euodia and Syntyche, both of whom he clearly loves and respects.
   - Verse 6—Paul tackles the problem of anxiety.

- **Clearly the situation in Philippi wasn't perfect or easy. So what do these verses tell us about how Paul views joy?**

Paul places his command between mentions of conflict and anxiety. He isn't waiting for ideal circumstances before he instructs the Philippians to rejoice. His command doesn't depend on the conflict getting resolved first or the Philippians overcoming their anxiety. Rejoicing is something we can do in the midst of difficulties like these.

- **If we are anxious about our lack of joy, what should we do?**

Verse 6 tells us that we need to present requests to God in prayer, with thanksgiving. We need to ask him to help us to carry out this command.

Explore More

- **What specific things is Paul rejoicing in as he writes to the Philippians?**
  - *1:4-6: His partnership in the gospel with the Philippian believers and his confidence that God will complete the good work he has begun in them.*
  - *1:18: That Christ is being preached, regardless of the motives of some of the preachers.*
  - *2:16-17: That his work will not be in vain if the Philippians hold firmly to the word of life, and that his imprisonment and probable death—like a drink offering poured out on an Old Testament animal sacrifice—will enhance their sacrifice and service for God.*
  - *4:10, 15-18: The Philippian believers have shown their concern for Paul by supplying his needs.*

- **What obstacles to rejoicing is Paul facing (or has he faced) as he writes? And what emotions could these situations generate that could threaten to undermine Paul's joy?**
  - *1:12-14, 20: Paul is chained somewhere in the imperial palace and*

doesn't know whether his imprisonment will end in life or death. *(Fear instead of rejoicing.)*

- *1:15, 17: Other Christian leaders are preaching the message of Christ out of rivalry with Paul and envy of him. (Betrayal, frustration or doubt in God's wisdom instead of rejoicing.)*
- *3:2, 18: The believers in Philippi are under threat from false teachers and surrounded by many who live as enemies of Christ. (Anxiety instead of rejoicing.)*
- *4:12-15: Paul has experienced times of need and hunger, and his experience of support from other churches has been disappointing at times. (Disappointment, anxiety or self-pity instead of rejoicing.)*

---

6. **What is it that most gives you joy? And how permanent is that joy? Could it be described as rejoicing in the Lord?**

Help people to answer honestly by giving your own answer first. Of course, there are many things in life that rightly give us joy, but Paul's command in Philippians is very precise (and deeply challenging): we are to rejoice specifically in the Lord and to do that always. Pray that people will start to talk about the joy they find in Jesus (or discover it for the first time) and that this will encourage others.

- **What have you learned so far in Philippians that would help you to grow in rejoicing in the Lord always?**

An opportunity to review what has helpfully struck people so far. In essence, we've learned that Paul's joy is not dependent on earthly factors; he sets his mind on heavenly realities, and so he has abundant cause for rejoicing.

7. **Read Galatians 5:22-23. What are the implications of Galatians 5:22 for how we think about joy as Christian believers?**

Joy is part of the fruit of the Spirit; at least three implications flow from this truth.

- Someone who has the Spirit will, among other things, grow in joyfulness. A continuing inability to rejoice must raise a question mark over any claim to have the Spirit (i.e. be a believer).
- We can't produce joy purely from our own efforts; we need the Spirit to work in us. And that means first we must be born again of the Spirit (John 3:3-5; 7:38-39; Acts 2:38; Romans 8:9b)—that is, become a believer in the Lord Jesus Christ. The Spirit works in us to draw our minds and hearts to truth about Christ so that we respond to him with understanding and faith—and joy.
- The joy of a Christian is distinctive and different from anything that people of the world might claim as joy. Because it's grown by the Spirit, it's only found in those who have the

Spirit. Whatever nonbelievers call joy will be something different—different in its source and unable to endure in all circumstances.

- **How does this make it possible to "rejoice … always", even in hard circumstances (Philippians 4:4)?**
When Paul commands the Philippian believers to rejoice, he's not thinking only of a natural response to pleasing circumstances, as most people define joy. To rejoice as Paul did is to be joyful in far-from-ideal circumstances. Typically it goes against our nature to find joy in unpleasing circumstances; we can only be like Paul because the Spirit grows this fruit in us. If joy had to be produced by our own effort, the command would be an impossible one.

8. **Read Romans 8:5-6. Look at what Paul says about a believer's mind. What similar things does he say about our minds in the Philippians passage?**
   - Philippians 3:18-21: He draws a stark contrast between believers, saved by the cross of Christ, and those who live as enemies of the cross of Christ. These enemies set their minds on earthly things—they intentionally think only about matters like how to fill their stomachs. But the believer has heavenly things to think about—our citizenship in heaven; our Saviour, who is coming back from there and who controls everything that happens to us; and our future

hope of bodily resurrection. Those are the kinds of things that we are to set our minds on.
   - 4:8: Paul tells believers to think about true, noble, right, pure, lovely, admirable, excellent and praiseworthy things. Again, Paul believes we can be intentional about the things we think about.

9. **How does all this (from questions 7 and 8) help us in following Paul's command to "rejoice in the Lord always"? What should we seek to do if we want to rejoice more?**
When our minds are full of wonderful true things about God and his people, we see reasons to rejoice. Note that the Spirit, who grows joy in believers as part of his fruit (question 7), does that through our minds (this question). As we set our minds on wonderful truths from God, the Spirit is at work in us, growing his fruit of joy.

10. **In the Bible, commands are given in the context of truth about God and promises from God. What truth (Philippians 4:5) and what promise (v 7) accompany this promise?**
The truth is that the Lord is near (v 5)—always. The promise is that the peace of God will guard our hearts and minds in Christ Jesus—the one in whom we are commanded to rejoice always.

- **How are the two connected?**
The Lord who is near (v 5) is the God who is the source of peace

and the Christ in whom his people's minds and hearts will be guarded by divine peace. The biggest factor that enables us to experience peace is confidence that the Lord is near; he has not forgotten or rejected us, and he is not stranded far from us and unable to help.

- **What do we need to do that will enable us to rejoice in the Lord always?**
  There's nothing that we must do to enjoy the Lord's nearness except to believe that. We enjoy the blessing of God's peace guarding our hearts and minds when, in every situation, we present our requests to God, particularly about things that make us anxious. Always and in every situation, the Lord is near to hear our requests, to replace our anxieties with his supernatural peace and to enable our joy.

  - *OPTIONAL: It's not possible to be joyful and angry at the same time. What evidence of rejoicing in the Lord does Paul point to here (4:5)?*
    Those who rejoice in the Lord are marked by gentleness in their character in a way that is evident to everyone around them.

11. **How have you seen the work of the Holy Spirit in your life, especially in growing the fruit of joy in you?**
    This question gives an opportunity for those who can do so to share about a time when the Spirit helped them respond with counterintuitive joy, showing that a believer's joy doesn't come from circumstances but from heavenly truths, in which we can rejoice whatever our circumstances.

Joy in Understanding God's Revelation

Nehemiah 7:73 – 8:12; Luke 10:17-24

The Big Idea

Joy is found in hearing and understanding God's word, especially as it is taught among his gathered people—a joy that we share with Jesus, who rejoices in the Father revealing to the minds and hearts of his "little children" all that he is and has done for us.

Summary

We begin our study in Nehemiah, not long after God's people, the Israelites, had returned to the land he had given them, following 70 years of exile that was imposed because of their rebellion against him. In the Old Testament, God's word was contained in the Law of Moses. So a key event occurred when the law was publicly read and explained to the gathered people, with the aim of producing understanding of God's law in all hearers.

The people first responded by mourning, weeping and grieving as they realised how shamefully they'd broken the law and turned against God. These were not just tears of disappointment at themselves; they were grieving, surely because of the ruptured relationship between themselves and the Lord. Their grief was evidence that they rightly understood something but also that they didn't understand all that God wanted them to—because they were not rejoicing.

Three times Nehemiah mentioned that the day of the gathering was holy to the Lord and therefore that the people should have been rejoicing and celebrating. Joy, not grief, was the appropriate final outcome of what they were learning from God's word. Through being told not to grieve, the people came to understand that even though they had broken the law, God wanted them to be filled with joy.

In Luke 10, as well as seeing Jesus teach his disciples the best thing to rejoice in (see Explore More), we are given a rare glimpse of what fills Jesus with joy himself (literally, making him leap for joy). It's the truth that God reveals himself in this fallen world, where everyone is born blind to God's truth (v 21). God reveals himself, Father and Son (v 22), in the way he chooses—through his Son (v 22). He accomplishes this in the people that he chooses (v 22), owing nothing to any human wisdom or learning (v 21), and with no regard to any human considerations of status or deservingness. All of this brings not only blessing to his chosen ones (v 23) but all of the glory to God alone.

Optional Extra

Try doing a lateral-thinking puzzle or a similar activity with your group. You can easily find some online. Ask any who know the answer to keep quiet and give the others a few moments to ask questions and try to work out the solution. When the answer is revealed, note the reaction of those who couldn't solve the problem themselves. It should be one of those "dawning light" moments. This is also something that people experience as they come to understand the good news of Jesus.

Guidance for Questions

1. **Share about a time when "the light dawned" and you understood something clearly for the first time (a subject at school, how to fix something, a sport or creative skill, realising how your significant other felt about you, etc.).**

   Encourage discussion by first talking about learning or discovering something that thrilled you—and about which you were bursting to tell someone.

• **Share about a time when "the light dawned" in your life as a follower of Jesus, and you understood something clearly about him in a new and powerful way.**

   Maybe it was when you first understood who Jesus really is—the Son of God, the only Saviour, really risen and alive today; or you grasped a gospel truth like grace or agape love or that God is the perfect heavenly Father of Christ's people; or you saw how the gospel applies to you personally—all your sins have been forgiven, you will rise from the dead, etc.

2. **What was the purpose of this gathering (v 1)?**

   To read the Law of Moses to all the people who could understand it.

• **Read Isaiah 49:6. How is this event in Nehemiah part of the fulfilment of God's promise to make his restored people "a light for the Gentiles"?**

   Miraculously, God's people were back in the land he had given them. And God had promised through Isaiah that he would then make them a light for the Gentiles so that his salvation would reach all people. So God's people needed to start living again under his rule—knowing, understanding and living out his word, which clearly they had forgotten during the exile.

3. **What point is made repeatedly throughout this passage (Nehemiah 8:2, 3, 8, 12)?**

   The law was read out so that the people would understand it. It was taught to all those who could understand: men, women and "others" (NIV) or "those who could understand" (ESV)—presumably children. This wasn't just a formal, ritualistic reading of their holy book; and that affected both how it was taught and what resulted.

- **How was the law of God taught?**
  - v 2-4: It was read aloud over several hours by Ezra the priest to all those who could understand.
  - v 5-6: It was read out in the context of praising God and showing him reverence.
  - v 7-8: Levites (temple servants) were also explaining it to the people. It seems they were dispersed among the crowd to speak to smaller groups and make the meaning clear.

- **How did the people respond to this opportunity (v 3)?**
  They "listened attentively", despite standing in the square before the Water Gate for a whole morning (v 1, 3, 7).

4. **What effect did hearing the law of God have on the listeners initially (v 9)?**
  They were weeping and mourning—also described as grieving (v 10).

- **Why, do you think? (Skim-read the Israelites' prayer in 9:5-35.)**
  Because, when they understood God's law, they realised its goodness (9:13) and how badly they and their ancestors had broken it (v 16, 26, 28-30). Their disregard of God's law had been the reason for Judah's exile (v 32-35). But they could also see how, throughout their history, God had always been faithful to his promises and full of grace towards his sinful people (v 7-8: Abraham; v 9-15: rescue from Egypt; v 17-25: the desert and the promised land; v 27, 30-31: the time of the judges, kings and prophets. God also forewarned them of exile and promised it would end after 70 years: Jeremiah 25:8-13 and 29:10).

  They were weeping over their failure and sin, but these were not just tears of disappointment at themselves; they were grieving, surely because of the ruptured relationship between themselves and the Lord.

5. **How did the leaders intervene (Nehemiah 8:9-11)?**
  They told them not to grieve. Instead, they were to enjoy feasting and share generously with others who had nothing prepared.

- **Why?**
  Three times we see that the leaders said the day was holy to the Lord (v 9, 10, 11). Grieving was incompatible with the holiness of the day. Though not wrong as a first response, it needed to be followed by joy and celebration as people grasped the marvel of God's goodness, faithfulness and grace.

6. **Look again at verse 12. Why did the people's response change?**
  They finally understood something more and better from God's word than their understanding in verse 8, which had resulted in weeping. They understood that in all his interventions—his law, prophets, leaders and teachers, promises, discipline, rescue and provision—God's intention was

not to grieve them but to fill them with the joy of the Lord.

- **How did they express joy?**
They enjoyed a feast together: gathering, preparing and celebrating together, along with sending out portions of food to ensure that everyone could join in.

7. **What emotional response do you typically associate with hearing God's word taught, and why? What practical lessons can we learn from this true story about how to find joy in God's truth?**
Encourage your group to share any obstacles they have to understanding and rejoicing in the teaching of God's word. Practical lessons from this story include…
- the importance of gathering with God's people to hear his word from specially gifted and commissioned leaders (v 2-8).
- the importance of giving time and attention to hearing God's word (v 3).
- the importance of coming to hear God's word with a worshipful mind and heart that reverence the Lord (v 5-6).
- the need to understand God's word and not just hear it (v 2, 3, 8 and 12).
- the importance of responding in penitence and grief over sin (v 9-11), but also…
- the further importance of growing into a deeper understanding of God that recognises how his holiness is displayed in his grace and

compassion as well as his righteous judgments (v 9-11).
- the rightness of celebrating joy in the Lord together with feasting and generosity (v 12).

8. **What was it, specifically, that gave Jesus joy?**
Jesus was exulting over the fact that his Father had revealed truth to the disciples—"little children" (v 21) and "those to whom the Son chooses to reveal him" (v 22): truth that was hidden from those considered to be "wise and learned" in society. Note how the Father and the Son work together to the same end: the Father reveals "these things" to the "little children" (v 21), and the Son does the same—he reveals his Father to those whom he chooses (v 22).

To summarise, Jesus was filled with overwhelming joy because, in this fallen world, where everyone is born blind to God's truth (v 21), God reveals himself in the way he chooses (through his Son, v 22) to the people he chooses (v 22). He accomplishes this owing nothing to any human wisdom or learning (v 21), without regard to any human considerations of status or deservingness. All this brings not only blessing to his chosen ones (v 23) but all of the glory to God alone.

9. **What humbling truth is revealed here about our understanding of God? How should we view ourselves?**
We cannot understand truth about

God unless he himself reveals it to us. Human wisdom, learning and worldly status are all useless for achieving this (v 21, 24). Even our longing to know who God is cannot help. We need revelation from God. And God chooses to reveal his truth to "little children". This is humbling—any understanding about who God is cannot make us proud.

10. **What exciting truth is revealed here about God's attitude to us in our ignorance? How should we respond?**
God is pleased to reveal the truth about himself to little children (v 21-22). His ultimate purpose is that his chosen people do see who he is, and he takes pleasure in opening the eyes of these "little children"—doing for them what they cannot do themselves. This is a beautifully reassuring depiction of God. As it did for Jesus, it should make us want to leap for joy.

11. **The fact that God reveals his truth to Jesus' disciples causes Jesus to "jump for joy"! This revelation is also available to us in Scripture (Ephesians 3:2-6). In fact, it is the foundation of the whole church (2:19-20). How will this affect the way you approach God's word and respond to it?**
People should be encouraged to expect a powerful revelation of God's truth from hearing God's word as it is read, taught, sung, discussed, recited and quoted among God's people, and to celebrate understanding it with great joy.

Explore More

NOTE: Luke 10:17-20 doesn't directly deal with joy in understanding God's revelation, but it shows Jesus correcting the disciples over where to find their joy and therefore tells us something valuable about Christian joy.

○ **How does the disciples' reason for joy (v 17) differ from what Jesus wants them to rejoice in (v 20)?**
The disciples rejoice over seeing the power of Jesus' name in compelling demons to submit to their commands, as they carry out Jesus' instructions to heal people (v 9). But Jesus wants them to rejoice that their names are written in heaven. (The next question explains this.) The disciples are thrilled at seeing the power of the Lord Jesus on earth, but infinitely greater joy is to be found in knowing and understanding their status before God in heaven.

○ **The image of a heavenly book or scroll with names "written" in it occurs throughout the Old Testament. What do the following verses reveal about it?**
• *Exodus 32:31-33: Moses is the first in the Old Testament to speak of such a book. Here, God is the only one who chooses to keep or blot out a name, and he removes a name as the penalty for sin against him.*
• *Psalm 69:28: Called "the book of life", God's book lists those who are righteous.*
• *Daniel 12:1: God promises future*

deliverance for those listed in his book.

- Malachi 3:16-18: God's "scroll of remembrance" lists those who fear and honour the Lord.

○ **What are the implications of our names being written in heaven?**

In the Old Testament we see people who are individually known by God, declared righteous and promised God's deliverance, and who fear and honour him. God alone decides who these people are. Jesus teaches his disciples to rejoice that they are counted among God's own people, each known to him and promised eternal life.

○ **How is Jesus' reason for joy a better one than the disciples', do you think? There could be many answers.**

- The disciples were rejoicing over what they could do in Jesus' name, but Jesus wants them to rejoice over what God has done for them.
- The disciples were rejoicing over earthly events, soon to be just a memory, but Jesus wants them to rejoice over their status in heaven— heavenly treasure that is eternally safe.
- The disciples were rejoicing over a display of divine power, but Jesus wants them to rejoice over an assurance of God's love.
- The disciples were rejoicing over the defeat of God's enemies, but Jesus wants them to rejoice over God's redemption of his people.

- The disciples were rejoicing over what they had seen with their own eyes, but Jesus wants them to rejoice over what they can trust God for by faith (compare John 20:29).

○ **The disciples overlook that reason for joy, and so might we. Why, do you think?**

The disciples had played a part in curing those afflicted by demons. This was no small thing (see Jesus' words in Luke 10:18-19): these miracles demonstrated how Satan had lost his power to the complete authority of Jesus over all his enemies. But God alone chooses and saves his people; only he can do it, and he does it with no contribution or deserving merit from us. This truth is totally reassuring for those named in God's book but also totally humbling. We naturally seek to justify ourselves, but we cannot, and we should not attempt to. Instead, we should rejoice in what God has done to justify us, as Jesus tells us to.

3

Joy in Repentance and Faith
Acts 16:16-34; Psalm 51

The Big Idea
Fear turns to joy when we first believe in the Lord Jesus Christ, and joy continues to be the fruit of repentance and faith in the life of a believer.

Summary
This session looks at how rejoicing in the Lord first becomes possible in a person's life. This study will be especially important if some in your group are not yet believers or self-identify as Christians but don't really know the gospel of Jesus Christ.

First, we investigate the story of the Philippian jailer in Acts 16. These events constitute the very beginning of the Philippian church—to whom Paul would later write his command to rejoice. The jailer heard the word of the Lord proclaimed by Paul and Silas in his prison, and he saw it lived out as they spent a night in the stocks praying and singing hymns to God, and as they declined to escape (along with the other prisoners, who had been listening to them) when presented with an opportunity to do that. We witness the jailer's repentance and faith as his conduct and attitude towards Paul and Silas change in response to their teaching of God's word, and we see the effect of that in him—he is filled with joy. He ends up displaying the standout characteristic that he witnessed in Paul and Silas.

Second, in Psalm 51 we see how sin will take away from a believer the joy of the Lord, but through repentance over sin and renewed faith the believer's joy is restored. This psalm of David, written after he had been confronted by Nathan the prophet with his sins of adultery and murder, gives us detail about what repentance and faith involve.

Optional Extra
Repentance and faith together form the right response to the good news of Jesus (Mark 1:15), so it's important to know what each means.

- Repentance = turning 180 degrees. See 1 Thessalonians 1:9 for a biblical explanation of repentance (turning from idols to serve the living and true God).
- Faith = trust. See Romans 10:9-13 for a biblical explanation of faith (believing in your heart that Jesus is Lord, that God raised him from the dead, and that you are saved by calling on his name—and publicly declaring that).

Split your group into smaller groups to do one or more of the following:

- Draw a diagram or picture of repentance and faith.
- Act out what repentance and faith are.
- Find a Bible example of repentance and faith.
- Work out a 60-second presentation to explain repentance and faith to someone who doesn't know these words.

Guidance for Questions

1. **What was it that gave you joy when you first turned to the Lord Jesus Christ in repentance and faith? (Or, if you grew up in a Christian family, when did your repentance and faith first lead to joy and why?)**

Answers might include:

- the forgiveness of sin—and relief from guilt.
- assurance of freedom from God's condemnation—and relief from fear.
- a sense of coming home to our perfect, loving Father—and relief from lostness.
- the thrill of having discovered what life is all about—and relief from meaninglessness.
- the certainty of knowing that our heavenly Father works everything for the good of his people, whom you have now joined—and relief from anxiety.
- the joy of a new start with new desires, hopes and ambitions, as part of the people of God—and relief from isolation and despair.

Share your own experience to help people get started.

(You might explain, for any non-believers, that all followers of Jesus have come to a point in their lives when they repented of their sins and put their trust in Jesus Christ to be their Saviour and Lord. All believers can speak of life before and after trusting in Christ, even if they can't remember exactly when that change occurred or it took place over a long period.)

2. **Why were Paul and Silas thrown into prison?**

They had rescued a slave woman by the power of Jesus Christ from a fortune-telling spirit and faced false accusations because her furious owners were unable to exploit her for money any longer. They were unjustly ordered to prison by a Roman magistrate after being stripped and beaten.

- **What obstacles had they encountered that might have dampened their joy?**

A vindictive response to their compassion (v 19); racism (v 20); outright lies about their conduct (v 20-21); mob attack (v 22); an unjust legal system indifferent to investigating the truth (v 22); severe physical violence (v 22-23); and degrading incarceration (v 23-24).

3. **What reasons can you think of to explain why—despite all that had happened—Paul and Silas could pray and sing hymns to God in prison? (See also Acts 5:41-42; 7:59-60; 13:49-52.)**

Connect answers with session 1: gather suggestions about what Paul and Silas would have set their minds on in the prison. Praying indicates faith in God and singing hymns their desire to express praise and joy.

(Refer to the other passages if people are stuck for ideas. Acts 5:41-42: Perhaps they were overjoyed to be counted worthy of suffering disgrace because of their allegiance and service to Jesus and his gospel. 7:59-60: Perhaps they were praying for forgiveness for those who had caused their suffering. 13:49-52: The filling of the Holy Spirit would enable them to respond to persecution with joy.)

4. **What was the effect of Paul and Silas's actions on the other prisoners (16:25, 28)?**
The other prisoners were listening to them (v 25). Undoubtedly, Paul and Silas took this opportunity to proclaim the good news of Jesus to anyone who could hear. When the earthquake opened the prison doors and loosed all the prisoners' chains, surprisingly no one tried to escape (v 28). We're not told why, but the implication is that this was the effect of Paul and Silas's testimony on their hearers.

5. **What immediate danger was the jailer facing, which might have provoked his question to Paul and Silas (v 30)?**
He might have been asking what he must do to ensure that he wasn't blamed and so probably executed for allowing his prisoners to escape. Or he might have been asking about how he could be saved from his sins as Paul and Silas had been.

• **What evidence is there to suggest that his question was in fact a spiritual one?**
  • The prisoners were not escaping; that's why he hadn't killed himself (v 27-29).
  • He listened to Paul and Silas as they explained how he could be saved from his sins (v 31-32).

6. **What's the evidence that the jailer responded to Paul's teaching both in repentance and faith?**
He humbled himself and served these prisoners by washing their wounds (v 33). Then he and his household, all of them having both heard the word of the Lord (v 32) and believed it (v 34), were baptised. Finally, he invited Paul and Silas into his home for a meal—a key mark of fellowship in the family of God (see Acts 2:46; 1 Corinthians 5:11).

• **What effect did this have on the jailer himself, and how did that contrast with the way he had felt previously?**
He was filled with joy (v 34). Previously, he had been full of fear (v 29).

○ *OPTIONAL: Events in this story could easily have caused guilt and fear in participants or observers.*
  • *The power of the Lord Jesus in freeing the slave woman from her evil spirit.*
  • *The unjust treatment of Paul and Silas, which so many played a part in.*
  • *The earthquake and its supernatural effect in the prison.*
○ *What fears should have been caused by each of these, and how would they have been relieved by believing the word of God, as the jailer did?*
Answers could include…

- *witnessing the mighty power of the Lord Jesus over his enemies—they would now know that same Jesus as their own Lord and Saviour.*
- *guilt over the part they might have played in the unjust treatment of Paul and Silas, all in sight of the sovereign God who intervened so powerfully to rescue his servants—they could now be forgiven through Jesus Christ crucified and resurrected.*
- *helplessness in the face of natural and supernatural forces over which they had no control—they could now understand something of God's sovereignty and his grace in Jesus Christ, and trust his control over their lives.*

7. What hints does the story give about how the jailer's life would change from now on (v 32-34)?

Everything listed here is characteristic of God's people in the New Testament church: proclamation and hearing of the word of the Lord (Acts 2:42); acts of service (1 Peter 4:10); baptism (Ephesians 4:5); fellowship and eating together (Acts 2:46); and joy (Romans 14:17). An embryo church was being formed in Philippi. Allegiance to Jesus Christ, his word, his mission and his people, and joy in the Holy Spirit would shape the jailer's life from now on.

8. The jailer was "filled with joy because he had come to believe in God" (v 34). Why might this be a surprising statement to some who don't follow the Lord Jesus Christ?

Many non-believers believe that God is only wrathful and judgmental, or distant and indifferent to them, or unknowable and incomprehensible, or well-intentioned but ineffectual, or tyrannical and repressive, or pointless make-believe at best and dangerous myth at worst. None of these views of God are inviting (or true); no one who holds them will think that believing in God brings joy.

• Why don't unbelievers equate repenting and trusting in Jesus with joy? Is there anything believers could do to remedy this? What could you do?

Non-believers often understand that following Jesus means giving up ungodly lifestyles and relationships but see nothing positive to make becoming a Christian worthwhile. Partly they are seduced by lies of the world and the devil and falsely enticed by their own desires, and only the Spirit can open their eyes and hearts to truth. But Christians often don't express joy in serving and following Jesus. We need to learn from the example of Paul and Silas and their open display of joy in prison. What an effective testimony for the gospel it was.

9. What has David discovered about himself (v 1-6)? Try to find at least five things.

Get people to answer verse by verse:
- He needs God's mercy (v 1).
- He has a record of transgressions

that need to be blotted out (v 1).

- He needs to be washed and cleansed because of his sin and iniquity (v 2).
- He can't forget his sin; it haunts him (v 3).
- David's adultery and murder have harmed many—Bathsheba; her husband, Uriah; the commander ordered to arrange the death of Uriah; the child of David and Bathsheba's union, who died; even members of David's family who suffered because of his compromised reputation (e.g. 2 Samuel 13). Even so, it is against God "only" that David has sinned (Psalm 51:4).
- So God's guilty verdict is right, and his judgment against David is just (v 4).
- David has been sinful his whole life, from birth—even conception. There was no doubt that David would grow to be a sinner (v 5).

None of this is good news. The most positive thing here is that God taught David wisdom in the womb (v 6), but that only underscores God's right judgment against David, who didn't utilise it.

10. **What will bring David joy again (v 7-12)? Try to find at least five things.**

Only God can bring David joy. Go through this section verse by verse to see how God can bring David joy again…

- by cleansing and washing him (v 7).
- by speaking to him in a way that brings joy and gladness (v 8).
- by turning his experience of anguish at how his sin has grieved and dishonoured God (likened to crushed bones) to rejoicing (v 8).
- by hiding his face from David's sins so that he no longer sees them (v 9).
- by creating a pure heart and renewing a steadfast spirit in David (v 10).
- by promising never to cast David from his presence or remove his Spirit from David (as he did from Saul; see 1 Samuel 16:14) (Psalm 51:11).
- by restoring to David the joy of his salvation (v 12).

- **What part does David play in any of this?**

None—these are all things that David asks God to do. This is David's faith in action.

11. **According to David, what does God delight in (v 13-19)?**

When we harbour sin and have not repented of it, God does not delight in our worship—which for David was an animal sacrifice (v 16)—even though he commanded it. Our outwardly correct worship isn't acceptable when we've committed blatant, egregious and intentional sin like David's. David first had to offer a broken and contrite heart (v 17)—to show true repentance and then faith, by turning to God to remedy his guilt and sinfulness. Only then would God delight in David's worship of him (v 19).

Explore More

○ *[1 John 1:5 – 2:2] What is different for God's people today?*

Jesus is the atoning sacrifice for our sins, not burnt offerings, which, though offered every day, had no power to make anyone righteous because they were only a shadow of what would come when Jesus appeared on earth (see Hebrews 10:1).

○ *What remains the same for God's people today?*

To be in right relationship with God and experience the joy of our salvation, we need to continually confess our sins and trust in Jesus to be forgiven and purified—just as David in Psalm 51 was repenting of his sin and trusting in God to cleanse him from sin.

○ *What reasons for even greater joy than David's does this passage give us?*

  • *The atoning sacrifice for sins today is not a dead animal but the living Saviour, Jesus Christ, who is also our advocate with the Father— speaking on our behalf and claiming us as his people, forgiven and made righteous.*

  • *His sacrifice not only achieves forgiveness of our sins but purifies us from all sin.*

  • *His sacrifice atones for the sins not only of one nation (ancient Israel) but of the whole world.*

12. **As believers in Jesus, what have we learned from Psalm 51 about how our joy can be lost but also restored?**

Like David, we all sometimes sin and lose the joy of our salvation—no longer delighting in unity and fellowship with the Lord Jesus. David shows how to repent (v 1-6) and exercise faith (= depend on God to work in us, v 7-15)—so that our joy in the Lord is restored (v 8), and then we will sing and testify about him (v 14-15). The sacrifice of a broken and contrite heart seems sad, but God delights in it as the sacrifice of a righteous person (v 17); it actually marks our restoration to a joyful relationship with him. So followers of Jesus need to continue as they started in the Christian life: repenting and trusting God for forgiveness—and as a result, rejoice!

• **Consider the three "movements" we've observed in Psalm 51: 1) owning our sin without excuses; 2) seeking forgiveness from the Lord; 3) trusting him to accept our repentance and delight in us. Which of those do you tend to struggle with most? Which verse from Psalm 51 would it be most helpful to hold on to in those moments?**

This is an opportunity for people to share something of their own habits of repentance, and where they struggle. Some of us struggle to see our sin and admit to it; others feel wretched but avoid God, rather than coming to him in prayer; others may pray and pray but still struggle with feelings of guilt.

4

Joy in the Lord
John 15:26 – 16:24

The Big Idea

To prepare his disciples for his imminent death, Jesus promises that he is going away for their good, that their grief will soon turn to joy, and that no one will be able to take that joy away—promises that persist for all whose joy is in the Lord.

Summary

In the final precious hours before his crucifixion (John 13:31 – 16:33), Jesus equips his disciples (minus Judas) to remain faithful to him and the gospel through and beyond the unimaginable events that are imminent.

He has told them repeatedly that he will soon be leaving them (see 13:33, 36; 14:2-4, 18, 25, 28-29; 16:5-7, 16). In this passage, now approaching the end of his teaching, Jesus addresses the grief that the disciples are already feeling over his departure.

By this point they believe he is going to the Father, but that prospect fills them with grief. Jesus wants them to see that he is going away for their good: namely, the Holy Spirit will come to them and do his work of convicting the world of the truth of the gospel and of who Jesus is. The Spirit will guide the disciples into all truth and equip them to testify about Jesus. Thus he will glorify Jesus. But before any of this happens, Jesus must die, rise and

ascend to heaven. Without these events occurring, the Spirit can't do his work.

The disciples understand that Jesus is going to the Father but still don't understand that he must die. To prepare them, Jesus makes four promises about joy:

- After he has gone for a little while (his death), they will see him again (his resurrection), and their grief will turn to joy.
- Using the illustration of a woman giving birth to a child, Jesus promises that what has caused anguish (childbirth / his death) will bring joy (a child results / atonement and salvation result).
- No one will be able to take that joy away from them.
- They themselves will then ask the Father for anything in Jesus' name and receive it, and their joy will be complete.

We too can have joy in the Lord without his physical presence on earth because the Spirit testifies to and through us that Jesus is proved—by his death, resurrection and ascension—to be the King of kings and Saviour of the world. The joy that nothing and no one can take away is to know him.

Optional Extra

To introduce Jesus' counterintuitive

statement in John 16:7 ("It is for your good that I am going away"), discuss how the following counterintuitive statements work.

- Don't search for happiness. (Happiness comes not when we're looking for it but when we're immersed in something we enjoy.)
- To be exceptional, don't believe you are exceptional. (Believe you can do better. People become exceptional because they understand that they're not, so they focus on improvement.)
- Limited choice is better than unlimited choice. (Too many choices paralyse us. Without other constraints, our responsibility for outcomes weighs heavily on us.)
- Irreversible decisions are better than reversible ones. (We adapt more quickly to consequences if a decision can't be changed. If other options remain open, we try to second-guess all possible outcomes.)
- Taking a risk might not be the riskiest thing to do. (People try to eliminate all risky activities from their lives but forget the risk of not doing something. The biggest risk might be to not take one.)

Guidance for Questions

1. **Share about a reunion with a loved one. What happened when you first met up? What had you most missed about them? What was different between video calls and seeing them face to face?**
Encourage those who have a story to share briefly.

2. **What is Jesus' purpose in speaking to his disciples at this time (16:1)?**
With unimaginable events imminent, Jesus spends these final precious hours equipping his disciples to remain faithful to him and to the gospel through and beyond his suffering.

- **What purpose has he previously mentioned in 15:11? How are the two purposes related?**
The purpose he has previously mentioned is that the disciples will receive his joy and therefore their joy will be full. The two purposes are related because joy fuels perseverance. That's why women can go through the hardships of pregnancy and childbirth (see 16:21, covered in question 10). Jesus will equip the disciples to persevere through the coming crisis by promising them that none of it will be able to destroy their joy.

- **To this end, what mission, promise and warning does Jesus give the disciples?**
  - Mission: To testify about Jesus (15:27).
  - Promise: That he will send from the Father the Spirit of truth with the same mission—to testify about Jesus (v 26).
  - Warning: That the disciples will be put out of the synagogue and even killed (16:2). He has already mentioned persecution in 15:18-21.
  - NOTE: Ejection from the synagogue also meant being treated as a pagan, leading to exclusion

from family and community, loss of income and suffering hatred and contempt.

3. **At this point, what do the disciples understand (16:5) and not understand (v 6-7)?**
   - Verse 5: They understand that Jesus is going to the Father. That's why no one now asks him where he is going, though they have previously asked this (see 13:36 and 14:5).
   - Verses 6-7: They don't understand how it can be for their good that Jesus is going away.

- **Why are they filled with grief?**
  Because they realise that Jesus will no longer be with them. They have a deep love for him; there's nothing better than being with him and nothing worse than being physically separated from him—especially in light of his statements about their future. They now know that when they testify about him, they will face extreme persecution; how can they do what Jesus asks without him alongside?

4. **In what counterintuitive way does Jesus address their grief (v 7)?**
   Jesus tells them that it is for their good that he is going away. The Advocate (the Holy Spirit—see John 14:26 and 15:26) will come to them, but Jesus is clear that the Spirit won't come unless he (Jesus) first goes away. The Greek word for "Advocate" is *paraklētos*: regularly used in New Testament times for a lawyer—someone who gives evidence that can stand up in court.

5. **What will the Spirit do when he comes (v 8-11)?**
   He will prove that the world is wrong about sin, righteousness and judgment. If your group want to think more about what this means, use the question below, or give a brief summary of the answer.

○ *OPTIONAL: How does the world think wrongly about sin, righteousness and judgment, and how does the Spirit prove them wrong?*
Sin (compare Acts 2:36-37): The traditional religious view of the time held that someone crucified was cursed by God and was judged to be a terrible sinner. Today people generally define sin as "not hurting others"; indifference to Jesus or rejecting him is considered irrelevant to sinfulness. But, as Peter preached, listeners were convicted by the Holy Spirit of their own terrible guilt in crucifying the one that God had made both Lord and Messiah, and people today are convicted of their indifference towards him. The Spirit reveals Jesus as the Messiah and therefore rejecting him as the ultimate sin.

Righteousness (compare Philippians 2:8-9): Paul shows how the resurrection and ascension of Jesus are God's stamp of approval on Jesus' self-giving love in becoming obedient to shameful death on a cross. No one else has ever risen from death and ascended to heaven; and only a perfectly righteous person could ever do so (Psalm 15). So through Jesus' resurrection and ascension, the Spirit reveals him to be righteous above everyone else.

Judgment (compare John 12:31-33): Jesus taught that his death would drive out the "prince of this world"; Satan would be defeated at Jesus' crucifixion; and those who remain part of this world are already under judgment (see also John 3:18). We tend to think we earn judgment if our wrong deeds eventually outweigh our good ones. But the Spirit reveals that as people of this world, born under the rule of its prince and under God's judgment, our only hope of escape turns on whether or not we come to believe in Jesus as the Messiah.

6. Why, then, must Jesus "leave" before the Spirit can come?

The crucifixion reveals that sin is to not believe in Jesus, the resurrection and ascension prove that Jesus is perfectly righteous, and all three events show the defeat and condemnation of Satan, revealing that his princedom—this world—is already under God's judgment. John Piper says, "[The Spirit] could not have come in full, Christ-exalting, gospel-applying, new-covenant-fulfilling, deepest sin-convicting, Satan-defeating power while Jesus was on the earth. No. The reason he couldn't is because every one of those hyphenated expressions, every one of those expressions of power, is based upon the death, resurrection, ascension, and rule of Jesus Christ. Those had to be done before the Holy Spirit could glorify them." (www.desiringgod.org/interviews/why-is-it-better-that-christ-went-away-john-16-7)

7. How does Jesus say the Spirit will help these specific disciples, and how will that help them in their grief (16:12-15)?

- Verse 13: He will guide them into all truth, in the same way that Jesus has; for example, he will not speak on his own (compare 7:16), and he will tell them what is to come (compare 16:2-4). For the disciples, it will be like having Jesus with them.
- Verse 14: He will glorify Jesus. No longer will their beloved Lord and Master be seen only as a mere rabbi or despised Galilean but revealed as the King of kings, promised Messiah and Saviour of the world.

8. When might you be tempted to regret Jesus' physical absence from this world?

Christians sometimes express wistfulness over living at a time when Jesus no longer walks on earth. This can be more deeply perplexing when we feel abandoned in tough times. Let people share at the level appropriate to each person, but since some may be suffering painful circumstances, don't insist on this.

- **But what would be missing today if Jesus had not physically left us?**
In effect, Jesus is saying that unless he

leaves (dies, rises and ascends back to heaven), there will be no life-giving gospel message through which the Holy Spirit can work to save and transform sinners and build the church. The Spirit's work—as the Helper and Advocate of believers (14:15-17), teaching and guiding into truth (14:26; 16:13), convicting the world of where people have gone wrong (v 8-11), bringing assurance of the enduring presence and love of the Father and the Son (14:16-21), and glorifying Jesus (16:14) and the Father (17:1)—all depends on Christ's death, resurrection and ascension into heaven.

- **Can you think of a time when, through the Spirit, you've particularly felt Jesus near? How did that bring you joy?**
  Encourage your group to share relevant personal experiences.

Explore More

o **[Song of Songs 1:1-4] How is the woman's joy expressed here?**
  In a desire to kiss the king—longing for intimate connection with him; in the contrast with the delights of wine and perfume; in the pride in others recognising his worth; in impatience to go away with him.

o **Where does it rank between feeling okay and ecstatic?**
  Right at the ecstatic end of the scale. No one can read this without sensing the joyousness of the love of the key players.

o **What is the source of joy in these verses—both of the woman and the chorus of friends?**
  Love between the woman and king—easily recognisable from the experiences or hopes and dreams of most people—and pleasure at seeing love flourish.

o **How does this speak to the relationship between Jesus and his people? (See Luke 24:27.)**
  In line with the biblical themes of God's plan for his people to be faithfully "married" to him and Jesus' wedding with his church at the end of history, this story can be read to give insight into the relationship between King Jesus and the people he has rescued. At its heart is love of the most profound, intense and joyous quality. This love—the idea and the intensity of it—can easily be appreciated by humans; the desire to experience a love like this, though distorted in multiple ways by sin, is hardwired into our creation design. The Bible's unique insight is that humans have been designed not only to enjoy love in all its perfections with each other but with Jesus too.

o **Do we have as much joy in Jesus as this woman has in her lover? If not, what might be the problem?**
  Perhaps joy is missing from a Christian's life of faith because love for the Lord is lacking.

- *How can we rekindle love for the Lord?*

  Only through remembering and revisiting his grace-filled love for us. Some may need to explore this for the first time.

---

9. **Reread Jesus' statement in verse 16. Which of his words particularly perplex the disciples and why, do you think?**

   They can't see how Jesus can go away only for "a little while" when he is going to the Father. The disciples must be thinking of Jesus returning to heaven and staying there until the end of the age. Jesus has spoken of this (e.g. 14:1-3, 19), but he also has in mind his imminent death (e.g. 14:30-31 [compare 12:31-33]; 15:12-13). Throughout this discourse he has been switching between these two departures. The disciples haven't yet understood that Jesus is also speaking of his death, so they are mystified by his words in 16:16.

10. **Jesus is preparing the disciples for his crucifixion by promising them joy (see column 1 in the table opposite). What four things do we learn about the joy that Jesus promises? (Complete column 2.)**

- **Later in the New Testament, how do we see Jesus' promises to his disciples regarding joy come true? (From the verses in column 3, complete column 4.)**

  See table opposite.

11. **Read Luke 24:50-52. How does Jesus' promise of joy come true just 40 days after his resurrection?**

   The disciples witness Jesus' ascension into heaven and respond with great joy and praise to God.

- **Why is the disciples' joy here surprising, and why not?**

  It's surprising because 42 days earlier the disciples were full of grief at this prospect. It's not surprising because it confirms that Jesus is who he has always claimed to be. He predicted his return to heaven (e.g. 16:5, 28), just as he predicted his death and resurrection (e.g. Matthew 16:21; Mark 8:31-32; Luke 9:21-22). He predicted that their grief would soon turn to joy; so it has turned out. He predicted that then no one would take away their joy. That couldn't be clearer now, as they see him ascending in triumph back to the Father.

12. **What have you learned from this passage that fuels your joy?**

   The key point should be that our joy is found in the Lord himself, whose triumph over sin, Satan and death—which his death, resurrection and ascension testify to—means that our joy can never be taken from us because our Lord lives and reigns for ever. Also...

- As we await resurrection, Jesus has not left us as orphans, struggling alone with testifying to the unbelieving world. His Spirit is convicting and convincing unbelievers through our testimony; mediating

John 16	Promise	NT Reference	Fulfilment
v 20	Grief is temporary and is followed by joy.	John 20:19-20	Three days after his crucifixion, Jesus rose from the dead. When he appeared to the disciples, they were overjoyed to see him.
v 21	In childbirth, the very process that caused anguish produces the child that brings joy. Similarly, Christ's crucifixion will ultimately bring the disciples great joy.	1 Peter 2:24	Jesus' death is the means by which we have been freed from sin (from its penalty and power now and someday from its presence)—so that we can now live for righteousness.
v 22	When their grief turns to joy, no one will then take away their joy.	Romans 6:5-10	In Christ, disciples are confident of a new life free from sin and alive to God, and of future resurrection, because Christ was raised and cannot die again. Nothing can take him away again, so nothing can take away all that is ours in him.
v 24	The disciples will then ask the Father for anything in Jesus' name. They'll no longer be limited to asking Jesus only when he's physically present with them— and their joy will be complete.	Philippians 4:4-7	Because of the Spirit, the Lord is always near (v 5; compare John 14:16-18). In every situation we can present requests to God (Philippians 4:6). When we do that, we are promised the peace of God to guard our hearts and minds in Christ Jesus (v 7). Thus we're equipped to rejoice always (v 4).

the presence of Jesus to us in all circumstances; and teaching and guiding us—until Jesus returns.

• Jesus did what he promised to do, and he's now where he promised to be—both with the Father and present with us by his Spirit. So how can we doubt that he will come back for us?

- **Where else, other than in the Lord, are you likely to look for joy? How does that compare with joy in Jesus?**
  An opportunity to remind one another that unlike anything else, joy in Jesus can never be taken away.

- **How could the truths from this study help you the next time you feel that you have lost your joy?**
  When we set our minds on these wonderful truths, we have marvellous reasons to rejoice.

5

Joy in Christ's Body

Acts 2:36-47; 1 Thessalonians 2:17 – 3:13

The Big Idea

There is great joy in the devoted fellowship of brothers and sisters in Christ, grounded in the hope, faith and love that are given to all who trust in Christ.

Summary

Right from the earliest days of the church, Luke tells us in Acts, believers in Jesus enjoyed fellowship with one another. The first church, formed in Jerusalem, consisted of people who shared life-changing experiences: accepting the message of Jesus, the crucified and risen Lord and Messiah; repenting and receiving forgiveness of sins; the gift of the Holy Spirit; and baptism.

Together, these first Christians were devoted to expressions of faith in Jesus that remain defining characteristics of any true church: the apostles' teaching, breaking of bread (see dictionary, p 34),

prayer and… fellowship. Their fellowship was expressed in showing hospitality towards one another, in regular and frequent meeting together, and in combining their resources to ensure nobody among them was left needy. And Luke's testimony is that they were sincerely glad in doing this.

The joy of Christian fellowship is highlighted by Paul's experience of his relationship with believers in Thessalonica. In 1 Thessalonians 2 he describes in surprisingly vivid language his feelings for the Thessalonian believers. The joy of his fellowship with them persists through troubling and frustrating circumstances because it is based on his hope in the return of Jesus and all that they will then be, as well as his faith in the Lord to supply all they need to reach that goal, and his gospel-fuelled love for them.

This session challenges us to find joy

in devoted fellowship with brothers and sisters in our church—fellowship that is grounded in the hope, faith and love given to us in Christ.

Optional Extra

Option 1 (if you belong to a sizeable and diverse church): True church is a remarkable gathering, and Christian fellowship with other believers gives us access to a far more diverse community in a far deeper way than most unbelievers will ever experience. Think about all the different people in your fellowship by answering these questions about your church:

- How many different decades are represented (0-9, 10-19 and so on)?
- How many different nationalities/ ethnicities are there?
- How many different occupations are there?
- How many different languages can be spoken?
- Can you think of any two groups represented that normally you wouldn't expect to mix (e.g. rival sports fans, nationalities with a difficult history, prison officer and ex-prisoner)?

Option 2: To accompany question 1, show video clips of crowd scenes at events like the 2023 UK coronation, the Boston Marathon, the Glastonbury Festival, the Notting Hill Carnival, 4th of July celebrations, Macy's Thanksgiving Day Parade or major sports fixtures, particularly scenes where a presenter is describing or asking about the atmosphere. Ask people to guess what or where the events are.

Guidance for Questions

1. **Why do you think people get so excited about the atmosphere at events where there's a large crowd? What makes experiences more enjoyable when we share them with others?**

If people are in any doubt about our modern-day fascination with "atmosphere", you only have to listen to outside broadcasts at a big event like the 2023 UK coronation; presenters repeatedly ask, "How would you describe the atmosphere?" and bystanders constantly refer to it to explain what they are enjoying most. People love feeling part of something "big"; there's a sense of unity even with strangers when lots of people enjoy the same event together.

2. **What had the people who formed the first church experienced in common with each other (v 36-41)?**

They had repented and received the gift of the Holy Spirit (compare John 3:5; Romans 8:9-11), as Peter had promised (Acts 2:38); they had been baptised and had joined the existing group of believers (v 41).

- **What does this role-model church teach us about what should happen next when an individual accepts the gospel?**

The normal pattern expected of new believers in the New Testament is that they join together with other believers. We don't follow Jesus as an isolated individual believer but as one among his people.

- **What does it teach us about what a church is—and who belongs to it?**
  A church is not just a gathering of anyone who fancies turning up; there's a process to go through before someone can belong to a true church: repentance; acceptance of the message of Jesus and trust in him as their risen Lord and Saviour; the gift of the Holy Spirit, seen in a changed life; and baptism.

3. **What four characteristics of a church are listed here (v 42)?**
   The apostles' teaching (now contained in the New Testament); fellowship; breaking of bread (see dictionary, p 34); and prayer.

- **What was the attitude of the believers to these things (beginning of verse 42)?**
  They devoted themselves to them. The Greek word for "devoted" means to persevere or endure—continuing to do something with intense effort—and can imply that this is done in spite of difficulties.

4. **How did the believers express their fellowship (v 44-46)?**
   They had everything in common and would sell property and possessions to provide for fellow believers in need. They met together every day in the temple courts. They broke bread and ate together in their homes. Though some details change later (e.g. where churches met, and how often), Luke's description gives a broad outline of what a church was expected to be throughout the New Testament.

- **How did they feel about their fellowship?**
  Luke mentions their "glad and sincere hearts" as they extended hospitality to each other. Their fellowship in the Lord was a joy, not a burden, and their joy was unfeigned, not fake.

Explore More

○ *[1 John 1:1-4] What is John's goal for his readers in proclaiming this (beginning of verse 3)?*
  He wants them to have fellowship with himself and the other apostles, which is why he proclaims the truth about Jesus that the apostles have witnessed.

○ *What other fellowship is produced by this message (end of verse 3)?*
  "Fellowship … with the Father and with his Son, Jesus Christ." Since John's purpose in proclaiming the message is "that you also may have fellowship with us", it's likely that when he then speaks of "our fellowship" with the Father and Son, he means that of both the apostles and the readers who accept the apostles' testimony.

○ *What is going to make John joyful?*
  The fellowship of believing readers with the apostles, and then the fellowship of all believers (apostles and

believing readers) with the Father and Jesus Christ. Fellowship in Christ, both horizontal and vertical, = joy!

---

5. How much would your fellowship with other believers in your church be recognisable to these New Testament believers, do you think? What are the differences?

If the discussion tends towards blaming others for lack of fellowship, point out that the question asks about "your fellowship". Focus the discussion on how Christians can contribute to wholehearted fellowship within their church in the ways practised by the Jerusalem church: sharing money and resources to eliminate need; meeting together, and not just on Sundays; and opening their homes to one another and eating together.

• **Is there anything you can do to help people in your church grow closer to resembling this first church?**

Some problems can only be addressed by those in leadership (e.g. a lack of Bible teaching). But you can lead by example in devoting yourself to fellowship and encourage others to do the same (e.g. opening up your home to fellow church members or showing hospitality in other ways like meeting in a cafe or park; or forming a prayer partnership/triplet to pray for each other and for church life and ministry). Encourage people, where possible, to invest time, effort and resources into their church fellowship.

6. In what ways does your fellowship with other believers in your church make you sincerely glad?

Start with your own example if people are slow to answer. Hopefully, positive answers from some will challenge or encourage others who struggle to appreciate church fellowship.

• **If this is lacking, might that be because you need to invest more in your fellowship? If so, how could you do that?**

Remember that the first Christians were "devoted" to fellowship. In our highly individualistic culture, we're tempted to pick and choose when we come to church and to opt out of commitments there, which would actually help us grow in fellowship. Half-hearted commitment means we won't experience the sincere gladness in fellowship that these first believers did. (People might prefer to think quietly about this question and write down action points privately.)

7. How many times does Paul mention "joy" in this passage?

Three times: 2:19; 2:20; and 3:9.

• **What exactly gives him joy?**

It's these believers and the prospect that they will be with him, blameless and holy, when the Lord Jesus returns. They will be like a crown for Paul—as if he were a champion athlete—and evidence that he has not run in vain the race of faith, service, sacrifice and endurance (2:19-20; 3:13).

8. **Paul's joy results from his hope. What hope is he looking forward to, and where do the Thessalonian believers fit in (2:19-20; 3:13)?**

Paul's hope is in the promised return of Jesus to earth (2:19; Acts 1:11), along with "all his holy ones" (1 Thessalonians 3:13), among whom Paul expects that he and the Thessalonian believers will be included. He eagerly anticipates celebrating in the presence of Jesus and enjoying his reward—joy and glory for him, for the Lord, and for all God's people, as everyone sees these once-pagan believers counted as "holy ones" (v 13) and welcomed into eternal life.

9. **Paul's joy results from his faith—in "our God and Father ... and our Lord Jesus" (v 11). What does he trust the Lord to do (v 8-13)?**

   - To keep the Thessalonian believers standing firm in the Lord (v 8)—the reason for his outpouring of gratitude to God (v 9).
   - To supply what is lacking in their faith (v 10)—one reason why he prays night and day for them.
   - To make it possible for him to meet them face to face, mentioned twice (v 10-11).
   - To fill them with increased and over-flowing love—the same love that he and his friends have for the Thessalonians (v 12).
   - To strengthen their hearts so that they will be blameless and holy on the day of the Lord's return (v 13).

   It's because Paul has faith in God to do all these things that he can have great joy in his fellowship with the Thessalonian believers.

   - **What thieves of joy does his faith overcome (v 2-5, 7)?**

   As we saw in session 1, Paul's joy persists in difficult circumstances. He himself has experienced trials and persecution since he last saw the Thessalonian believers (v 3-4). He fears they will have been unsettled in their faith by hearing of these trials, and that the tempter will have used this as an opportunity to tempt them away from living for Jesus. His "distress" (v 7) probably refers to intense anxiety about them. But since Paul has confident faith that the Lord will provide all that the Thessalonians need, his distress has been alleviated by the joy that he is testifying to.

10. **Paul's joy is linked with his love for the Thessalonian believers. How does he express that here (2:17, 19-20; 3:5, 8, 9, 12)?**

    - He feels "orphaned" by being separated from them (2:17).
    - He has an "intense longing" to see them (v 17).
    - He has made "every effort" to see them (v 17).
    - They are his hope, joy, crown and glory (v 19-20).
    - Paul couldn't stand not knowing how the Thessalonians were progressing in their faith, and he was fearful for them (3:5).
    - "Now we really live": Paul celebrates the fact that their faith has stayed firm (v 8).

- He doesn't know how to thank God enough for all the joy he feels because of his fellowship with them (v 9).
- His love for them overflows, just as he prays that their love for each other and everyone else will also overflow (v 12).

11. How has Paul invested in his fellowship with the Thessalonian believers (2:17; 3:1-2 and 5-6, 10-13)?

- He has made every effort to see them in person (2:17).
- He preferred to be without Timothy in Athens, sending him to Thessalonica to strengthen and encourage the believers and report on how they were doing (3:1-2 and 5-6).
- He prays "night and day" and "most earnestly" for them, asking God to provide what they need, make it possible for him to see them again, grow their love and strengthen their faith, and keep them faithful until Christ returns (v 10-13).

12. How do you think your fellowship with other believers compares with that of Paul and the Thessalonians? How much is it based on the faith, hope and love that are ours in Christ? (Or does it centre around something else?)

Perhaps think about the following:

- How often do you pray with a fellow believer?
- How often do you read a Bible passage together or talk about something you have learned from God's word?
- How often do you ask someone how they are doing in their faith?
- How many stories of coming to faith in Christ do you know from among fellow believers?
- How often are you fearful for the faith of someone in your church, leading you to pray earnestly for them?
- How often do you feel joyful about being with your fellow believers when the Lord returns?

If none of these occur very often, it's likely that your fellowship with others in church is not in the Lord but in something else—compatible personalities, interests, experiences or stage in life. That's not what Paul is describing, and it won't result in the deep, enduring joy that Paul experienced from his fellowship with these brothers and sisters even in distress and persecution.

- **Paul seems to have written his letter from Athens (3:1); the fellowship of believers from whom he was separated was very important to him. How could you grow in fellowship with believers who live elsewhere?**

One great Christian joy is fellowship with Christ's people around the world. Are there missionaries, churches or organisations that your church supports from whom you could hear about believers elsewhere? Discuss how to show these brothers and sisters love: e.g. praying and advocating for them, fund-raising, sending video messages, visiting, etc.

6

Joy in Suffering
Luke 6:17-36

The Big Idea

Joy in suffering sounds like an oxymoron, but Jesus promises that, because of our reward in heaven, as his followers we are blessed even though now we are also poor, hungry, weeping and rejected—so blessed that even in persecution we can leap for joy.

Summary

In his famous sermon recorded in Luke 6, Jesus makes some astonishing statements about those who are his disciples. At this point, Jesus is still popular among the people who come to hear him and be healed by him, so surely everyone would expect his disciples also to enjoy popularity and success. And Jesus does call them "blessed". But in the same breath, he describes them in ways that no one would consider enviable or helpful for happiness: as hungry, poor, grief-stricken and persecuted.

Jesus can insist that his disciples are blessed because he has brought us into the kingdom of God; so we're heading for joy, when hunger will be filled, grief will turn to laughter, and we will receive a great reward. We can begin to experience that joy now, first, by looking forward to our reward; and it's such a great one that we can leap for joy, whatever is going on in our lives. And second, by looking back, we can be reassured in persecution because we're following in the steps of earlier faithful believers.

The key difference between Jesus' disciples and the people of this world is that his disciples are willing to suffer now for the kingdom of God because of faith in the promises of God and the hope of our eternal reward—whereas unbelievers only live for happiness now. It's that same future orientation that enables disciples of Jesus to reflect the character of our heavenly Father in our interactions with unbelievers and enemies of the gospel.

Optional Extra

Share with the group one or more stories of Christians persecuted for their faith in Jesus. For recent stories, see, for example:

- Voice of the Martyrs:
  www.persecution.com/stories
- Open Doors:
  www.opendoorsuk.org/news/stories

Get people to guess which country each story comes from. Or pause partway through a story and ask people to predict what happens next. Or maybe members of the group have a story they wish to share. Note: Such stories can be very moving so be prepared. Some might contain distressing details, so think carefully about the people in your group who may have particular sensitivities e.g. people who have suffered trauma, pregnant and post-natal women, under-18s, or migrants, asylum seekers and refugees.

Guidance for Questions

1. **Think of a time when you persisted with something that was painful or stressful because you knew that the outcome would make it all worthwhile. How did you feel along the way and in the end?**

   For example: study and exams; sports competitions; physical challenges like mountain climbing or marathons; physical or mental rehabilitation; living in a different culture; and so on. This question highlights how we could already be familiar with something of what Jesus is speaking about in Luke 6.

2. **Look at the description of Jesus' ministry in verses 17-19. What might people expect life to be like for Jesus' disciples?**

   Many from far and wide have come to hear Jesus teach and be healed of troubles caused by evil spirits and illnesses. Jesus appears both popular and successful, so it would be natural to assume his disciples were also going to enjoy popularity and success.

3. **What does Jesus expect life to be like for his disciples (v 20-23)?**

   Jesus describes them as "blessed" (see dictionary, p 39). But in the same breath he describes them in terms that no one would consider enviable or helpful for happiness.

- **List all the kinds of suffering that he mentions.**

   Poverty, hunger, grief and rejection—meaning they will suffer hatred, exclusion, insult, slander, blame and shame.

4. **According to Jesus, in what ways are his disciples blessed amid all this suffering?**

   - Theirs is the kingdom of God (v 20); though poor now, through Jesus they have joined God's kingdom—a treasure that cannot be destroyed because it is not part of this world (Matthew 6:19-21), and one that is worth giving up everything for (13:44-45).
   - They won't remain hungry; one day they will be satisfied (Luke 6:21).
   - They won't weep for ever; one day their weeping will turn to laughter (v 21).
   - Because they have been rejected and persecuted, they will receive a great reward in heaven (v 23).

- **How does Jesus describe their joy in looking forward to their reward in heaven (v 26)?**

   He says they will "leap for joy". And they will be able to do that "in that day"—the day when they are being hated, excluded, insulted and rejected as evil. As we saw in session 2, this phrase describes an overwhelming exultation. Jesus' statement here is a remarkable combination of two things that are usually considered incompatible. You could ask in what circumstances people have ever leapt for joy.

NOTE: Jesus' reward of his faithful people is mentioned many times in the New Testament (e.g. see the Sermon on the Mount, Matthew 5:11 – 6:18; 10:40-42; 16:25-27; 1 Corinthians 3:6-14; Ephesians 6:7-8; Colossians 3:22-24; Hebrews 11:6; Revelation 22:12). See Revelation 22:1-5 for a description of God's reward to his faithful servants.

5. Jesus' followers will be helped to persevere through suffering by keeping their future in view. What view of the past will help them too (v 26)?

Disciples should understand that they are being treated no differently from earlier faithful prophets of God (v 23). Persecution can be a badge of honour, showing how we follow in the steps of the godly faithful of previous generations. This suggests that it's important to know the history that Jesus refers to. Ask people to name Bible figures persecuted for speaking God's truth or acting according to it (e.g. Abel, Genesis 4:1-8; Gideon, Judges 6:25-30; Jotham, 9:1-21; Ahimelek and the priests of Nob, 1 Samuel 22; Elijah, 1 Kings 19:1-3a; Elisha, 2 Kings 6:24-33; Jeremiah, 20:1-2; 26:1-11; 38:4-13; John the Baptist, Mark 6:17-29).

6. Jesus' disciples have a focus on the future. What is the focus for those in verses 24-26? And so, what is the chief characteristic that Jesus is looking for here?

The godly faithful are willing to suffer now for the kingdom of God because of their faith in the promises of God and the hope of his eternal reward. Unbelievers are not willing to give up present pleasures and popularity for an eternal reward.

- **Why should we not envy the people described in verses 24-26?** Because everything they treasure most is passing away and will soon be lost to them, leaving them with an eternity of nothing but woe.

Explore More

- *How does the writer of the book of Hebrews make the same point as Jesus in Luke 6?*
  - *10:32-39: The first readers of Hebrews had themselves suffered persecution previously, either directly themselves or alongside other believers. They accepted this with joy because they knew they had been promised far better things in eternity.*
  - *12:2-3: Jesus himself endured the ultimate shame and suffering of the cross because of the joy that was set before him—the joy of what the cross would eternally achieve in the salvation of his people and in glorifying the God of grace and justice.*
  - *12:16-17: By contrast, Esau prioritised the short-term pleasure of a single meal over the permanent but then-distant blessing of his spiritual inheritance as the eldest son. He regretted his short-sighted*

but irreversible decision. His story strongly warns us today against prioritising temporary pleasure over the permanent reward of eternal life.

- *13:11-14: The writer exhorts readers to willingly suffer disgrace for Christ, who was so disgraced at his crucifixion. Again, we can do this because we are not looking to make our home in this world but in the world that is to come.*

---

7. **How are you encouraged to persevere in faithfulness to the Lord through tough times by looking back to history (including Bible history) or looking forward to eternity? Talk about people and events (from the past) or promises (for the future) that have particularly helped you.**

Be ready with your own examples if the discussion is slow to get going.

8. **Jesus is speaking these words to "you who are listening" (v 27). Who are these people (v 20) and can you summarise Jesus' message to them in one sentence?**

Jesus seems to address "you who are listening" in contrast to the people he's just described in verses 24-26. The listeners are faithful believers—those described in verses 20-22. In summary, Jesus tells them that the hardship and opposition they face now because of him will result only in blessing one day.

9. **What practical differences can be seen in someone's life when they trust Jesus' assurance that his followers are blessed in suffering?**

Jesus gives them a list of instructions that are just as counterintuitive as verse 23:

- Love your enemies and do good to those who hate you (v 27).
- Bless and pray for those who try to harm you.
- Offer someone a fresh start (turn the other cheek) when they abuse you (v 29).
- Show generosity and don't insist on your rights when people take what is yours (v 29-30).
- Treat others as you would wish to be treated (v 31).
- Lend to people without expecting any repayment or return (v 34-35).

These instructions are impossible, even incomprehensible, for those not trusting in Christ. But those who place all their hopes in God's eternal reward of his faithful servants are called and enabled to act in ways that reflect the character of our heavenly Father. You could ask your group to share how they've seen such behaviour in the lives of believers they know.

10. **What is the ultimate reward that they will receive (v 35-36)?**

Jesus promises those listening to him in verses 20-36 that they will be children of the Most High and share the character traits of their Father (v 35-36). Here's the crowning point of all that Jesus has been saying: our greatest reward is that we will grow to become like our heavenly Father himself in his mercy and grace.

11. **"To you who are listening I say..." (v 27). What is it that stops us from truly listening to Jesus in this area?**
    - Things that hamper us from hearing Jesus—e.g. we're too distracted by other priorities or we've got out of the habit of joining with church to hear God's word.
    - Things that stop us from trusting Jesus—e.g. the present seems more real or more satisfying than our promised eternal future. Of course, the two answers are related: when we lose the habit of letting God's word speak into our lives, we struggle with unbelief.

- **Why might we struggle to trust that we are blessed when we are suffering for him?**
  Some may have wrong expectations—they think that faithfulness to the Lord should be rewarded with deliverance from persecution and the defeat of gospel enemies now. Or they lack assurance that Jesus has won an eternal reward in the presence of our heavenly Father for all who trust him.

- **Why might we feel unable to be kind to the ungrateful and wicked, as our heavenly Father is?**
  It's mostly when we forget or have never realised that we have been ungrateful and wicked ourselves. When we grasp how much we need God's mercy and how freely he has forgiven and saved us, we want to be like him and show the same love to others that we've received.

- **How are we helped by doing these things alongside one another?**
  It's important to realise that God does not call us to live this way by ourselves. (See Explore More: the Christians mentioned in Hebrews who suffered persecution did so together, with those not directly targeted standing alongside those who were.) Among God's people, we can see and imitate those who love their enemies, we can encourage one another with Scripture, we can pray for one another, and we can share both the burdens of grief and the delights of joy.

7

Joy in Hope

1 Thessalonians 4:13-18; Revelation 7:9-17

The Big Idea

Our hope in Christ—of the Lord's return, bodily resurrection, the new creation, and eternal life together with God our Father and Jesus our Shepherd, free from sorrow—is the heart of Christian joy. To treasure this hope as our goal is the sure recipe for indestructible joy.

Summary

Without a sure hope that cannot be overcome by death, joy is only temporary; natural sources of joy in this world will be lost to us when we die. True, lasting joy must encompass a rock-solid hope that not only survives but disarms death.

In 1 Thessalonians 4, the apostle Paul outlines just such a hope. The first-generation Christians he writes to are eagerly awaiting the return of Jesus (1 Thessalonians 1:10), but they are concerned about Christian brothers and sisters who have already died. Believers seem to be dying just as non-believers die. What has happened to them, and what will become of them if they are not here when Jesus comes back?

So Paul reveals what will happen when Jesus returns: he will bring with him those believers; they haven't truly died but their spirits have been waiting with him for the end of the ages while their bodies have been asleep (see dictionary on p 45). Those dead in Christ will rise first, and each soul will be reunited with their resurrection body. The bodies of believers who haven't died will be instantly changed into imperishable resurrection bodies, and they will be caught up together with all the others to meet the Lord in the air. From that moment, all of Christ's people will "be with the Lord for ever" (4:17). The effect of this hope is that though Christians grieve when a believer dies, they don't grieve "like the rest of mankind, who have no hope" (v 13).

In Revelation the apostle John shows something of what being "with the Lord for ever" will be like. He describes a multitude of God's people "that no one [can] count, from every nation, tribe, people and language" (Revelation 7:9), worshipping God our perfect Father and Jesus our Shepherd; and all pain and sadness will be gone. The effect of this hope is that the joyousness of what lies ahead makes all our troubles now seem light and momentary (2 Corinthians 4:17).

Optional Extra

Hope quotations quiz: Get people to guess the words missing from these quotations about hope. Help people out by giving a clue: the first letter of each answer, or jumbled answers, or anagrams or multiple-choice options. End by voting on the best/worst quotes or ask which people agree or disagree with.

1. Alexandre Dumas: "All human wisdom is summed up in these two words: _____ and hope." (wait)

2. Martin Luther King, Jr: "We must accept finite _____, but never lose infinite hope." (disappointment)

3. Charles M Schulz: "A whole stack of _____ never equal one little hope." (memories)

4. Fyodor Dostoyevsky: "To live without hope is to cease to _____." (live)

5. William Shakespeare: "The miserable have no other _____ but only hope." (medicine)

6. Napoleon Bonaparte: "A _____ is a dealer in hope." (leader)

7. Emily Dickinson: "Hope is the thing with _____ / That perches in the soul / And sings the tune without the words / And never stops at all." (feathers)

8. The Bible: "But those who hope in the Lord will renew their _____." (strength— Isaiah 40:31)

9. The Bible: "'For I know the plans I have for you,' declares the Lord, 'plans to prosper you and not to harm you, plans to give you hope and a _____.'" (future— Jeremiah 29:11)

10. The Bible: "May the God of hope fill you with all joy and peace as you trust in him, so that you may _____ with hope by the power of the Holy Spirit." (overflow— Romans 15:13)

Guidance for Questions

1. In what different ways do people in your culture hope they will "live on" after their death?

In the secular West, it's about how people remember you. Fame and noteworthy achievements are the greatest "hope" for living on in people's memories, but most of us will have to suffice with being remembered by a few relatives and friends that outlive us—until they also die. People work to leave legacies such as an inheritance for their children, foundations and charities, memoirs and scrapbooks, and so on. Popular religious or sentimental beliefs in some sort of afterlife—a new star in the night sky, looking down from above—don't bear much scrutiny.

• How well or badly are these hopes likely to fare?

Memories of people—even famous people—fade within two generations. A hundred years after our death, probably no one will remember us.

2. What concern among the Thessalonian believers is Paul addressing here?

People can work this out from what Paul is telling the Thessalonians here. They are concerned about Christian brothers and sisters who have died before Jesus' return to earth. They see no difference physically between believers and non-believers; believers are dying just as non-believers die. What has happened to them, and what will become of them if they are not here when Jesus comes back?

3. **List all the things that Paul mentions will take place when the Lord Jesus returns.**
   - The Lord Jesus will come down from heaven to earth again, announced by a loud command, the voice of an archangel and the sound of a trumpet. (See Acts 1:11; Jesus will return from heaven in the same way that he left.)
   - Jesus will be accompanied by the souls of those who have fallen asleep in him (1 Thessalonians 4:14). Compare 2 Corinthians 5:6-8; Paul describes only two alternatives for believers before Christ returns: either living in our body and away from the Lord (here on earth) or away from the body (because it has died) and at home with the Lord (our soul with him in heaven).
   - The dead in Christ will rise first (1 Thessalonians 4:16)—their dead bodies will be raised as imperishable resurrection bodies that are reunited with their souls (see 1 Corinthians 15:52).
   - Those believers still living on earth will be caught up together with all the other believers to meet the Lord in the air (1 Thessalonians 4:17). At that moment their bodies too will be instantly changed into imperishable resurrection bodies (see 1 Corinthians 15:51).

   - All of Christ's people will be with him for ever (1 Thessalonians 4:17).

4. **Therefore, what should differentiate believers in Christ from unbelievers?**
   We can grieve with hope; when fellow believers die, we do not grieve over them like "the rest of mankind, who have no hope" (v 13). Note that Paul doesn't tell the Thessalonians that they shouldn't grieve but that they shouldn't grieve like people of this world. Also note how it is possible for a believer to be both sad and joyful at the same time.

- **How is the joy experienced by unbelievers undermined by their lack of hope?**
   Any joy can only be temporary. Nothing that causes them joy will survive beyond death. When loved ones die, they are left only with hopeless grief. When they themselves die, they leave behind everything that has given them joy.

5. **When and where have you witnessed hope-filled joy among Christians in the face of death? What effect did it have on others?**
   There is something very powerful about a Christian funeral, where people are not afraid of grief but do not give way to despair, and where they can share their hope in Christ with assurance and even joy. Have an example ready to share if people are slow to contribute.

6. **What key things does John tell us about the people of God in eternity (v 9)?**
   - They are a great multitude that no one can count.
   - They come from every nation, tribe, people and language.
   - They are wearing white robes and holding palm branches (see dictionary on p 47).

- **How can these things cause us joy now, as we wait for this reality to arrive?**
  - *A great multitude.* Often the church of Christ in this world seems small and weak. But John's vision assures us that God's plan for his kingdom involves a vast number of people, just as he promised Abraham centuries ago (see Genesis 13:16; 15:5). We needn't be discouraged by our weakness or insignificance because God's plan will prevail.
  - *From every nation.* Many people deeply desire peace and unity between nations and cultures and feel frustration over barriers caused by different languages and histories. This longing will be met in the church of Christ in eternity, but even now diverse ethnicities and cultures united in church can give us great joy.
  - *White robes and palm branches.* Many things cause God's people to feel defeated: opposition and persecution, our own failures, fellow Christians lapsing into sin, those who fall away from the faith, betray-

als and disappointments; but John's vision assures us that a victorious outcome for God's people is not in doubt, so we have great reason for joy even in these troubles.

7. **What do the two songs or declarations (v 10 and 12) reveal about the reasons for joy in eternity?**
   - Verse 10: God's people recognise that their salvation is solely due to the desire, will, plan, sovereign power and costly grace of God through the atoning death and triumphant resurrection of the Lamb. Nothing and no one else can take any credit for salvation, which is what makes our salvation fully effective and secure. Notice the words "our God". All of creation rightly acknowledges God as Creator, but for God's saved people there is a special bond. God is our God—our Father (Matthew 6:9) and our Saviour (Jude 1:25). God and his saved people belong together.
   - Verse 12: Attributes that are fully true of God alone (glory, wisdom, power and strength) are mingled with the responses that are rightly due to God (praise, thanks and honour) from all created beings. These things are true or sure ("Amen!", said twice) for ever and ever. The whole picture, with God and the Lamb at the centre and worshipped as such, is one of eternal security—everything as it should be and nothing ever able to threaten any of it.

8. **Compare what we are told about life for God's people in this world (7:14) with how their life in eternity is pictured (v 15-17).**
   - **What is different?**
   In this world God's people (those who have "washed their robes and made them white in the blood of the Lamb", v 14) experience the great tribulation. Some commentators believe that "tribulation" refers to a limited period of intense trials for Christians that will occur immediately before the return of Jesus (see Matthew 24); others believe it means all the trials suffered by God's people throughout history, as predicted by Jesus. (Compare Jesus' warning to his followers in John 16:33, using the same Greek word as Revelation 7:14—"in this world you will have trouble".) The Greek word means not only persecution (as in Acts 11:19) but also "suffering" and "anguish" caused by circumstances such as famine or childbirth (Acts 7:11; John 16:21), and both external and internal troubles (as experienced by Paul in 2 Corinthians 7:4-5). But in eternity "never again" will God's people suffer any of these troubles (Revelation 7:16), and even the memory of them will not distress them as "God will wipe away every tear from their eyes" (v 17).

   - **What is the same?**
   God's people serve him. God shelters his people. The Lamb is their Shepherd. In other words, we will have the same wonderful relationship with our God.

Explore More

○ *[Isaiah 25:7-9] Look at what God will do, and where (v 7-8a; 24:23). What does this add to our understanding of God wiping away our tears?*

Isaiah prophesied that "on this mountain" (Mount Zion or Jerusalem; see 24:23) God would destroy the shroud that covers all peoples and all nations—namely, death. The prophecy was fulfilled when Jesus died on a cross in Jerusalem as the atoning sacrifice for the sins of the world. Through his death, God's people enter new life that will last for ever. There will be no more tears in eternity because there will be no more death.

9. **What two relationships are central to John's vision of God's people in eternity (v 17)? What do you find particularly striking about them?**
   - First, the Lamb will be our Shepherd. He's already our Shepherd (see John 10:2-3, 11, 14), but this role will not end when he has led us into eternity; he will continue to shepherd us, leading us to springs of living water. In eternity Jesus will still be the provider of all that we need, and we will enjoy it all perfectly.
   - Second, God will be our perfectly loving Father, as seen by the universally understandable picture

of wiping away our tears. It's an image of gentle intimacy; this will be the eternal unclouded reality of the relationship between every saved human and their sovereign, almighty, all-holy Creator. Again, God is already the Father of his people in this world, but in eternity we will relate perfectly to him as his precious loved children.

- NOTE: Perhaps some in the group have never understood that, at heart, the Christian faith is about reconciliation and a restored relationship with God through Jesus Christ. Instead, they view the Christian faith merely as a way of living a good life or escaping from judgment or earning a reward in the next life. While all of these perspectives are true, they miss the heart of the gospel—and of eternity. A good test of understanding is to ask: what is it about Christian hope that gives you joy even in tribulation? People might mention seeing a loved one again or the end of pain and difficulty. But no mention of the joy of being in God's presence or the thrill of meeting Jesus face to face strongly indicates that someone lacks a full understanding of the gospel.

10. **Read 2 Corinthians 4:16-18—our hope of eternal glory far outweighs our troubles and makes them seem light and momentary. How can we help each other to remember our hope so that we persevere in the faith with joy, even in troubles?**
This is why Jesus calls his followers to gather together; we need to encourage one another with reminders of our eternal hope. Part of participating together in the Lord's Supper is proclaiming the Lord's death "until he comes" (1 Corinthians 11:26). When we have close relationships with one another in God's family, we can see and imitate brothers and sisters whose Christian hope gives them joy to persevere through tribulation.

11. **As this is the final session, spend a few moments writing down and then sharing what has given you most joy in learning about joy over these studies.**
Give people a few moments to flick back through their booklets before sharing their answers.

Explore the Whole Range

Old Testament, including:

New Testament, including:

 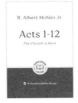  

Topical, including:

Flexible and easy to use, with over 50 titles available,
Good Book Guides are perfect for both groups and individuals.

thegoodbook.com/gbgs
thegoodbook.co.uk/gbgs
thegoodbook.com.au/gbgs

the good book

COMPANY

BIBLICAL | RELEVANT | ACCESSIBLE

At The Good Book Company we are dedicated to helping Christians and local churches grow. We believe that God's growth process always starts with hearing clearly what he has said to us through his timeless and flawless word—the Bible.

Ever since we opened our doors in 1991, we have been striving to produce resources that are biblical, relevant, and accessible. By God's grace, we have grown to become an international publisher, encouraging ordinary Christians of every age and stage and every background and denomination to live for Christ day by day and equipping churches to grow in their knowledge of God, their love for one another, and the effectiveness of their outreach.

Call one of our friendly team for a discussion of your needs or visit one of our local websites for more information on the resources and services we provide.

Your friends at The Good Book Company

thegoodbook.com | thegoodbook.co.uk
thegoodbook.com.au | thegoodbook.co.nz
thegoodbook.co.in